THE FIGHT OF YOUR LIFE

THE
FIGHT
OF
YOUR LIFE

Clive Calver & Derek Copley

KINGSWAY PUBLICATIONS
EASTBOURNE

ISBN 0 86065 355 2

Unless otherwise indicated, biblical quotations are from
the New International Version, © New York International
Bible Society 1978.

Front cover photo: Tony Duffy, All-Sport Photographic Ltd.

Printed in Great Britain for
KINGSWAY PUBLICATIONS LTD
Lottbridge Drove, Eastbourne, E.Sussex BN23 6NT by
Cox & Wyman Ltd, Reading.
Typeset by CST, Eastbourne.

Contents

I

Appointment with Harry

I could just picture him sitting there. Pen poised in hand, chewed end, running his left hand through his thick, curly brown hair. Furrowed brow and intense expression of pain on his face. It was always hard for Harry to admit that he was wrong, especially when he had maintained for so long that his was the only tenable position and that I could only be kidding myself.

Young enough to be my son, I always had a certain sympathy for Harry. He was too honest not to be likeable and I grinned to myself at what it must have cost him to write this particular letter.

Suddenly I was sitting bolt upright. Now that's not a normal position for me while I'm reading the mail on a Saturday morning. I much prefer the lazy way of doing things. Relaxing in the most comfortable armchair, catching up on the postman's contribution to a weekend of leisure. This was a different Harry—his words had spilled on to the paper—writing as if he were sitting in the room speaking to me face-to-face. The contents of that letter finally penetrated, I let out a whoop of joy and turned to read again.

Don't ask me why I went. I haven't got a clue, but I

suppose all my study, training and discussions over the years demanded fair play. After all, anyone deserves a hearing, so there wasn't really any choice. Then my repudiation of his bland, smug, self-satisfied brand of conservative hogwash would have complete integrity. After all I'd have heard him for myself.

I'd known Harry for a long time. It's hard to say that anyone actually 'knows' Harry anyway. All the same, we had spent long nights sitting on the floor of his poly-technic bed-sit, drinking coffee and talking through the early hours. Subjects and topics licked on from one to the next, the usual menu being Jesus, hunger, strikes, the bomb and Harry himself!

Four or five hours on his floor was about par for the course. Once a term I would arrive to address a motley bunch of students and there, sitting on the back row, would be Harry. He always hoped that nobody would notice him. Ashamed to be there, reluctant to listen to what I had to say, yet ready and waiting to whisk me off into a one-off debate stretching way into the night.

I read on.

Have you ever experienced that sudden sense of some-one out there speaking to you? Not a Doris Stokes, or some vague telepathy, but a clear recognition that things are happening and words are coming through which should be rejected—but somehow the excuses aren't real any more. It's as if your whole life is passing before your eyes. Past, present, and forgotten episodes in a sequence of images flashing into your mind. Behind it all a sense of unutterable uselessness. A surprising con-viction that somewhere, somehow I just might have missed it!

I could hardly believe it. Could this be Harry, the tall, happy-go-lucky, freewheeling thinker whose easygoing brand of moderate socialism fitted in so perfectly with my own. At first I had been so certain that our conversations and friendship would lead to the commitment of his life to Jesus Christ. Somehow it never quite happened. He wasn't antagonistic—just totally committed to intellectual neutrality. Every six weeks or so his conscience would prick him and a letter would be fired off in my general direction. The contents would include an offer of space to sleep should I be passing, apologies for wasting my time in fruitless conversation and a restatement of his latest mental conclusion on the last piece of verbal repartee. Harry's state of mind seemed permanent, immovable. Spiritually everything was quiet on the western front! So certainty gradually became a vague hope which in turn faded to a passive resignation in the face of the seemingly inevitable. Harry would always be interested but it could never go any further!

The trouble was we never seemed to arrive at conclusions—Harry didn't really believe in getting answers; his preoccupation lay in the most appropriate phrasing of the question. Like so many people, he was quite happy to concede religious belief as a private habit. What one person finds essential to their well-being, another person can do without. One person goes to church, another plays golf. Each should do what he feels to be right for himself, without inflicting his own viewpoint on others.

Putting my reminiscences firmly in the background, I turned again to Harry's letter.

At least thirty thousand people were in the stadium. It seemed so vast. How could he discuss 'You and God' with everyone else around? What could be so universally relevant that it would draw a crowd? Anyway, there we all were, singing old hymns and simple religious ditties. Then the longest prayer that I'd ever heard. Then a song before the American spoke. Now you know what

I think about pious Yanks preaching to British sinners. Thing is it was cold that night. I knew I should feel really uncomfortable but I began to feel warm inside. It seemed really strange. Almost a sense of déjà-vu in fact. I'd heard the man's message before, it was almost an echo of all our late-night conversations.

This was the first indication I had had that any of my comments about Christianity or Jesus had registered with Harry. There was a sense that I was the only Christian that he really wanted to talk to—perhaps because one monologue, one letter, and one conversation a term was about the limit to his openness on the subject.

Still, Harry was genuine and likable, and there were constant reminders of many who were very patient with my own enquiries before I finally committed my life to Jesus Christ. Besides, who knows, a foundation might be laid—and God has a habit of surprising all of us!

Certainly the level of shock was explosive that morning. I read his letter with mounting excitement. Somehow I knew in the pit of my stomach exactly what was coming next!

It was so straight and so simple. Sinful man separated from a holy God who longed to share his life with them but faced up to a seeming permanent barrier. Only God's love and his own self-sacrifice would cleanse away sin. The positive response would be repentance on man's part and forgiveness on God's. Suddenly I saw it all! Jesus physically dying on the cross to remove my separation from God. He alone could form the bridge by which I could come to God—so that he could live in me. Yes, I know you told me so often. But that night it was different. Standing on the turf looking up at the speaker I knew I'd done the impossible. I'd walked forward as a statement that I wanted to give my life to Jesus Christ!

I almost laughed—I'd told him that so often! In fact the very words which he used to describe what he'd heard were almost word for word my own. Moreover, they were words which Harry had so often dismissed as irrelevant to him.

I'm not readily emotional but I felt tears stinging my eyelids because I knew how often I'd dreamed of this moment. Harry had great potential. His talents could make him a tremendous warrior for God. It's so often the way, those who seem most unreachable have the most to offer. Behind his hostility lay a sensitive articulate personality. He was a man who would never suffer fools gladly and one who would make a clear straightforward stand for truth—once he'd discovered it!

So there I was just standing there. I could hear him praying. I just knew that I couldn't really help myself. All the reservations, all the arguments and fears just drained out of me. In my heart I couldn't escape the fact that I knew I'd been wrong.

It must have cost a very great deal to write those words. Like most people he never liked facing up to the fact that he might be wrong. I realized above all that the letter itself was a fantastic confirmation of all that had now begun in his life.

Joy and apprehension flowed over me in consecutive waves. No one other than God's Holy Spirit could have achieved this amazing transformation. Yet I knew from the bottom of my heart that it would have to be only the first of a multitude of miracles for Harry ever to develop into a mature Christian.

Then I saw that there were several more pages to the letter—and I knew with a sense of foreboding that things were not going to be easy from now on!

I always thought that once I'd taken the step, then every-

thing would come together—my doubts, fears, and questions would all disappear.

Problem was—they didn't.

I had a pretty good idea of what had begun in my life, I'd surrendered my heart to Jesus Christ but now I found that my head was giving me all kinds of problems—so I went to church.

Now I did what you'd suggested all those months ago. I tried the nearest church where they actually believed the Bible. How's that for a controversial statement! Anyway I walked in and everyone was friendly, apparently they'd been told about me by the system from the mission. So the only surprise was that I'd got to them—before they reached me!

Well, I pigeonholed the minister after one of the services. I just treated him as if he were you. Anyway I started chatting about 'wet Christians', 'mindless belief', you know, the usual sort of thing. The poor guy nearly blew a fuse! The trouble was that he thought all my problems should have disappeared too!

That vicar had my sympathy! Knowing Harry, I could imagine what a nasty culture shock the poor man must have received! Harry didn't know how to just 'accept things'. Each new concept and situation had to be up for examination and open to question.

I did my best to pour cold water on to Harry's fears but my reply lacked conviction. I recognized that, against the rules though it was, Harry really needed an 'honest broker', who was not connected with his church, to whom he could talk. So that's the offer which I made. Any time he needed answers but recognized that the shock of the question might create confusion in his local situation—then I was quite happy to be a sounding-board.

It didn't stay there! Harry never knew the meaning of standing still. His natural enthusiasm took over and he

went for broke! At the same time I moved to the north
of England and it was not so easy to meet. So instead of
talking we began writing. Conversations on paper have
their drawbacks. It might take a week to answer one
minor point. By that time Harry had gone on to the next,
and the next, leaving no time to deal with the big issues.

That's how this all started. Ever since he'd taken his
stand on the wet turf of the football stadium and begun
talking to a gentle, concerned counsellor Harry had
known that he couldn't deal with it all by a cautious,
patient, rational approach. He needed someone to lash
out at—and I was his victim!

By this time Harry had completed his polytechnic
course and had joined the world of the workers! An
office job was scarcely his cup of tea, but he worked
away at it. It did give him plenty of opportunity to talk
about his faith, and it certainly raised enough issues for a
voluminous correspondence.

So his letters grew longer and so did mine. In the end
he wrote:

> *It's all taking too long—but I know that I'm growing in*
> *God. What I need is to get answers to the big and basic*
> *questions. What about forgetting the short for the sake*
> *of the long? If you could respond in treatise form to any*
> *problems or areas of concern then I can think through*
> *what you say.*
>
> *I never need the heavy stuff, I can read that up, but*
> *the normal practical approach would be really helpful.*

Harry never thought about all the work that would
entail; Harry never thought like that. But I suppose he
never guessed that I'd get a book out of it at the end of
the day. Still, Harry wouldn't mind that. By this time he
had begun to realize that he was by no means unique!

2

Don't You Know There's a War On?

No, I don't think I've suddenly packed in Christianity. I defend Christian belief, standards, the Bible and all that. It's not that I've become totally disillusioned, but I do feel real disappointment.

Somehow there is a shallowness both in logical thought and in the life style of many of the Christians whom I've begun to get to know. Compromise is everywhere. It's all become too easy—and the rationalizations for the 'acceptable' styles of behaviour just flow like water from a tap.

Anyway, I stuck it out for a few days and then went to see the vicar to try to work it all out. I scribbled some notes, tucked them in my pocket and went along to the vicarage. Both he and his wife were really warm and welcoming—we drank tea, and then they asked what my problem was. So I let them have it! I posed three questions:

1. I've read that Jesus claimed to be unique—why then do church leaders and congregations alike challenge that claim? It's not just notorious characters like the Bishop of Durham. I read in a Christian newspaper the other day about a 'Christian' rock star announcing that his Hindu friend, who believed in Jesus and Mary along with all his other gods, was quite all right. His statements were never even challenged! It seems that we Christians are so scared of offending people, and of seeming bigoted, confident and arrogant—getting up people's noses—that we've totally lost our nerve. Jesus, it seems, is no longer the only way to God but just one among many. If, of course, everyone isn't saved automatically anyway!

2. If Jesus called us to be salt and light in a wild and restless world—why do we just sit at home and content ourselves with going through the motions? Many of the Christians I've met recently seem to live lives which are little different from those of everybody else.

Magazines, records, meetings, books, parties, friends —but they're all 'in house'! It's the same lifestyle as the rest of the world but emerging from a Christian sub-culture which concentrates more on income than integrity.

3. Ninety per cent of my generation live in complete ignorance of the Christian message. How do we justify our lifestyle and attitude in terms of lobbing the odd strategically placed mortar bomb in the general direction of a mankind rushing to its own eternal destiny? On Sunday we preach the gospel to the converted. The rest of the week we try to beat the world at its own game. Then we claim that prosperity and success are the best demonstrations of the truth of Christianity? I really don't understand.

By the time I'd put the last question the atmosphere had changed. What's more, the vicar's face had gone a little chalky! I nearly laughed. Like my honesty disturbed him and he wasn't used to being questioned.

So he started to talk about none of us being perfect. Then he went on to suggest that it's hard to live up to the truth. He even claimed that it was unfair to look at the church and one should examine the life of Jesus instead.

But how can you look at Jesus if the rest of what Paul called 'his body', the church, isn't living up to scratch? It makes a nonsense of Christianity if all it adds up to is a set of ideals which no one has to achieve. So I left the vicarage and thought I'd drop you a line. I know these questions are too much all at once—so how about starting with this one?

You often used to tell me that the Christian life was a battle. That Christians had to live up to their message— but what's wrong with keeping your nose clean, staying out of trouble, and putting your feet up at home?

*   *   *

We are at the front. In the front line. And this front line is all around us because the enemy has surrounded us on all sides. We are surrounded by the godless. There is not a single place which is free from attack—the press, art, the theatre, schools, official institutions, everything is occupied by the godless. The laws are designed to suffocate religion. We've been at the front for a long time.

Those words are not drawn from the latest futurist melodrama; they come from an orthodox priest broadcasting out of the Soviet Union in 1977. Such oppression should not come as a surprise. Jesus promised us life 'with persecutions' (Mark 10:30). Throughout large areas of Eastern Europe conversation about God is actively discouraged; where church worship is permitted it finds itself under rigid, institutional controls; religious festivals are ignored, or replaced; a policy of imprisonment of church leaders aims at the neutralization of Christian leadership.

The fact remains, however, that in the East persecution has done little to hinder the growth and spiritual development of the church. Once again the words of Tertullian, the second century church historian, have been proved correct: 'The blood of the martyrs is the seed of the church.' Fantastic growth in small house church congregations within China and Eastern Europe only parallel the flood of converts being gained by evangelical Christianity in South-East Asia, Africa, and Latin America.

You made your own commitment to Jesus Christ in a football stadium filled to capacity with people wanting to know about Jesus Christ. But such events are rare in western Europe.

Such good news is not popular in the contemporary western mind, with its bias to cynicism and scepticism. Our own brand of press and media censorship has prevented ordinary people in the West from even being aware that we live in the middle of what is numerically and geographically the greatest move of God which this world has ever seen!

Persecution in the West is of a very different order to that in the East. Rather than taking the form of overt opposition it is of the subtle, insidious variety. Dull apathy, empty churches, the façade of respectable adherence—'I'm C of E'—all contribute to deny to the church a powerful role in society. Most people retain a small compartment of their lives for what they call Christianity —but it's no more than a word to them. They're devoid of genuine conviction.

Sociologists tell us that there has been a massive rejection of institutional Christianity on the part of most people. Less than one per cent attend church today in the East End of London. Some sixty per cent of all churches and missions have closed in the past twenty-five years.

A close friend of mine had been visiting church leaders in an Eastern European country. At the end of his trip one of the senior leaders encouraged him by giving an assurance of regular prayer but added a word of warning: 'Please tell our brothers and sisters in England that we are praying for them as well, because we know that they are not living as God wants them to!' One morning we will perhaps wake up to the reality that a massive struggle has taken place over the tortured body of the church in Western Europe. The results are already devastating—but tragically many Christians have not even noticed! We recognize the problems of the communist East, but ignore the greater tragedy on our own doorsteps.

This is a most important discovery which you've arrived at. You're beginning to ask my favourite question for Christian friends. It's very simple:

Don't you know there's a war on?

A calm and gentle breeze drifts across the church in western Europe. Occasional ripples spread across its bland surface. The odd internal argument, emergent new cult, doctrinal emphasis or cash-flow problem, disturbs the scene for a moment or two . . . but quickly passes away. New organizations and initiatives emerge, old ones continue, evangelism becomes a special effort in the life of the church. Gossip and criticism are quick to fill any vacuum in evangelical conversation. Little change . . . little growth . . . and little impact on the population whose comment on Christian credibility has been made with their feet.

Don't you know there's a war on?

Compromise

The temptation is, of course, to admit defeat, to give way under the pressures, to gently bend in the direction that the wind is blowing—but the results of such action can be absolutely devastating.

(a) The habits of society are whitewashed and the laws of God are ignored. So a 'Gay Christian Movement' can emerge with 'evangelical gays', in the face of all that Scripture says in forbidding homosexual practice.

(b) Christian acquiescence is exhorted in the face of

the most flagrant disobedience by rulers and government of the laws of God. So when the Warnock report leaves open the possibility of genetic experiments involving the implantation of semen from animals into the human female ova we are supposed to just sit there in passive acceptance!

(c) It is considered perfectly acceptable to pour mockery and scorn on to Christianity, yet Hindu, Moslem, Buddhist, humanist and Jew are all protected from blasphemy and insult. Christians, however, have to endure a gradual erosion of all that is important to us. The other day I was listening to the football results. The match reports followed. A prominent player was being interviewed. His comments went, 'God, it was great.' 'Christ we were lucky.' If he had said, 'Buddha, it was great. Muhammad, we were lucky' there would have been a national outcry! But anything, it appears, is acceptable when referring to the Lord of Glory, Jesus Christ. In fact many have remarked on the way in which 'God' and 'Christ' have become the two most common expletives within our contemporary society.

In many senses of the word, God couldn't be more public! Not as King of kings but in a blasphemous empty phrase, an easy going good-luck charm, as someone to be blamed or congratulated according to our every whim or fancy.

When a famous athlete married his childhood sweetheart she arrived twenty minutes late for the wedding. He explained to TV newsmen, 'I thought, O God, the car's broken down!'

Everybody's talking about God. We may live in an increasingly secularized society but the divine names constantly crop up, in everyday conversation, in business discussions, on school playgrounds and in the media.

Just as Jesus had to remind the Samaritan woman of her heritage and reveal to her who the one was that she found herself talking to—so we have a similar responsibility today.

The danger lies in our attempt to kid ourselves that there is plenty of time left. 'Hell' has been discredited as a concept in our modern world. After all, if God loves us, how can he separate people from him for eternity? When we stop living in the light of the judgement seat of Christ we cease to recognize that sharing the reality of Jesus is drawing people back from a godless eternity.

Your heart is beginning to cry out for a positive, militant Christian lifestyle. Such sentiments are not terribly popular today. Too often Christians rarely act as if they are a people at war. Too often we'll do anything, and turn a blind eye to any situation, in order to keep the peace. In the face of a hostile world we largely stay silent. Fear of accusations of fanaticism or eccentricity prevail. But what would you do if the name of your wife or mother was used as a constant curse? Why then do we stay silent?

Don't you know there's a war on?

Celebrations

Good Friday is no longer a national holiday. The meaning of Whitsun is largely forgotten, Christmas increasingly becomes a celebration to the great god, Materialism. If the baby in the manger is remembered, it is in an orgy of drunken sentimentality or commercial carol singing. Are we Christians going to take stock and recognize what is happening?

Two men were reading the church poster, 'Put "Christ" back into Xmas'. One turned to the other and commented, 'Cor, they try to get religion into everything, don't they?'

Next Christmas shepherds and wise men will be remembered. Yet one event of the Christmas story sandwiched between those two visits will be ignored, as it is each year. Shepherds and wise men greeting a baby boy as Son of man is acceptable. What we choose to ignore is the twin testimony of Simeon and Anna that this was no mere mortal baby but Son of God; man as man should always have been, God as God always will be, here on earth as a baby. No wonder Simeon responded, 'For my eyes have seen your salvation, which you have prepared in the sight of all people' (Luke 2: 30–31). It turns me back to the cry—don't you know there's a war on?

Concepts

It is very easy to look back to a bygone Christian era; to a time when the nation honoured and served the Lord. Unfortunately, historians have still not managed to trace this golden age! Our nation has never been truly 'Christian'; equally, it has rarely managed to treat God quite so casually as now. At a time when the church of Christ in Britain faces perhaps its most demanding time of trial, it writhes in the throes of a massive crisis of confidence. Many would maintain that evangelicals in the nation are suffering a chronic loss of nerve. In a day which cries out for clear leadership, for men and women who will go out on a limb with God and challenge the nation to turn again to God, few are prepared to recognize, let alone accept, the task of the hour.

It is all too easy to argue that the protests of one or two individuals will achieve little, to claim that my voice would never affect anyone. But Jesus himself taught that faith that is small, like a grain of mustard seed, can become very influential indeed. Into this wilderness of silence has come the quietly ordered voice of John R.W. Stott.

What, then, should Christians do? We should seek to educate the public conscience to know and desire the will of

God. The church should seek to be the conscience of the nation . . . In evangelism we should neither try to force people to believe in the gospel, nor remain silent as if we were indifferent to their response . . . In social action, similarly, we should neither try to impose Christian standards by force on an unwilling public, nor remain silent and inactive before the contemporary landslide . . . We therefore need doctrinal apologetic in evangelism (arguing the truth of the gospel) and ethical apologetic in social action (arguing the goodness of the moral law.) Apologists of both kinds are wanted urgently in today's church and world.

Issues Facing Christians Today (Marshalls, 1984)

At the bar of public opinion an emasculated, reminiscing and confused church pleads 'not guilty' to rocking the boat or challenging the norms of our contemporary social order.

Again the echo comes in prophetic tones to you and me, and to the largely passive, silent, majority of evangelical Christians today: 'Don't you know there's a war on?'

Changes

For too long the church has concentrated its attention on internal change. Concern for our own situation has diverted our gaze from the realities of a dying world. While we discuss the advisability or otherwise of hands being raised in the air above shoulder height during a worship service, an opposition is wielding the axe of radical change:

The vast majority of evangelical Christians were not even aware of the private member's bill in the 1960s which abolished the prohibitions on witchcraft.

A leading women's monthly magazine employs its own psychic columnist to peddle 'spirit messages' to its readers.

An exhibition of human depravity and torture from a

historical perspective started to incorporate a range of occult exhibits. School-children invited!

A Radio 1 Disc Jockey offers a two minute lesson on how to levitate!

A Christian youth club was denied its local authority grant because it advertised for a 'Christian' youth worker. It was admitted that to have specified 'Buddhist' or 'Rastafarian' in the advert would have been perfectly acceptable.

For years General Booth fought to raise the age of consent to sixteen, today the battle is on to reverse that decision.

The world is deafened by our silence.

Don't you know there's a war on?

Sadly, the problem is largely of our own making. While society has silently rejected Christianity, we have submerged ourselves in our own Christian subculture. Gazing inward, to our own records, meetings, books and magazines, we have inoculated ourselves against infection from the world outside. Our passion for Christian events and activities has absorbed every spare minute, leaving us no time to face the real world. At the same time our instincts for battle have been turned inwards on each other.

Isolation has never been the answer. Jesus lived his years on earth confronting his society, and we have no grounds for spiritual pacifism. We will never make the world go away by pretending that it doesn't exist. Turning a blind eye to a sinful society will not guarantee us a safe and untroubled stay on this earth. Burying our heads in the sand never changed anything.

Jesus stated that such indifference and complacency is wrong. Light and darkness can never peacefully co-exist; one must always triumph. If we live as the light from God in the darkness of a pagan world then eventual victory is secure. 'The light shines on in the dark, and the darkness has never mastered it' (John 1:5 NEB). One Roman Catholic housewife challenged the entire weight of the Health Service over doctors' refusal to tell parents when they prescribed contraceptives to minors. One small protest and a leading chain-store removed hundreds of thousands of magazines containing an anti-gospel article.

What is needed is a new generation of Christians. Men and women utterly devoted to Jesus Christ, committed to a vision of the King and his kingdom, recognizing that spiritual warfare is not, in the main, a matter of occult activity. Men and women committed to a day by day overcoming of personal temptation to live the life of Jesus in victory through the power of his Holy Spirit.

> And souls grow weary in this war of love
> And seek their solace strolling down the sweet civilian ways.
> Graham Kendrick, *God Put a Fighter in Me*, © Thankyou Music 1978.

Christians are needed who will recognize, as the apostle Paul did, that Christianity is a battle, not a picnic. After all, 'No-one serving as a soldier gets involved in civilian affairs—he wants to please his commanding officer' (2 Timothy 2:4). When soft Christians begin to recognize this fact then society and state alike will begin to feel the force of lives destined to turn their world upside down.

Such people will face up to the tragic loss of morale which afflicts the church. Their lives will be lived in the world to the glory of God. Their words will be a challenge and encouragement to fellow-believers. Their attitudes will divide between truth and unbelief so that long-forgotten spiritual militancy—courage for the things of God—will be recovered in our day and generation. Graham Kendrick continues in the same song:

> Where have all the Christian soldiers gone?
> Where is the resistance, will no-one be strong?
> When will we stand up tall and straight
> Rise up and storm the gates?

Such people will not hide in the face of either a challenge or an enemy. They will rise up in confidence that the living God has conscripted them for his service and has both the power and authority to use them in overcoming all the wiles and ploys of the opposition.

> How can we fail to get excited?
> The battle is ours, why don't we fight it?
> Battalions of darkness rise above me
> But God put a fighter in me.

Spiritual militancy might well seem to be considerably 'over the top' in the pale light of much of the Christian activity in the western world. But to the early church, or to our brothers today in much of the so-called 'third world', it is normal. God has always wanted an army which would stand for righteousness and justice, but whose weapons would be godly lives, compassion and the word of God. Today is no time for spiritual pacifism. God grant you the courage and strength to begin to be a fighter for truth, justice and the Lord Jesus within this nation. You may be surprised to find how much I agree with you, but these concerns, for a faith that is vibrant, real and can face up to the future has always been at the heart of the message of Jesus.

> Listen and you'll hear the sweetest sound
> You ever heard in England.
> It's the Spirit moving across the land,
> It's the voice of one who calls his bride
> To come and to be ready.
> Gentle as a dove, He comes with fire.
> Where have all the Christian soldiers gone?

Don't you know there's a war on?

3

Heading for a Fall

*That essay you sent—I don't know what else to call it—
it certainly rang so many bells that I felt in the middle of
a belfry! Talk about sparking off all kinds of trains of
thought! It's been helpful and has put things into perspective. At least I now know that if I'm a heretic there's
two of us around!*

*I feel that it has helped me to understand a lot of the
reactions from fellow Christians. At least I feel far more
positive than I did when I wrote that last letter.*

*You never quite realize when looking at Christianity
from the outside how easy it must be to begin with
enthusiasm but gradually slip back into just 'going
through the new motions'—while keeping up the old
lifestyle! Now I'm noticing more and more how safe my
fellow Christians seem to feel. If all that radically
changes in their lives is the addition of Bible-reading,
churchgoing and praying along with the deletion of a
few bad habits then theirs isn't the Christianity for me.*

*That's a roundabout which I don't want to drift on
to. It's just getting nowhere. I won't ever consciously
fall into that trap but I'm afraid of it happening without
my even realizing what is going on.*

I set myself specific aims and objectives. I'll do this or that, spend time here or there, but whenever I fail to achieve my own targets it seems so simple to just pass that off as inevitable. I recognize that there's a war going on, what I'm uncertain about is, who exactly is the enemy? Is it just this materialistic society? Or am I the enemy myself? Until I've identified the opposition I'm not quite sure how to cope with the situation.

On top of that, if I'm not my own worst enemy, then why have so few others seen that the battle is real—and so is the opposition! How do I recognize where the conflict is taking place, and how much is it all a convenient excuse for my own problems?

Sorry, the thoughts are confused, but it's an area which seems really grey, and I'd certainly appreciate some black and white inserted into it! No one's given me any straightforward answers—some have warned me to avoid the 'demon-seekers'; others have cautioned me not to humanize the supernatural and one Christian actually suggested that I'd soon get used to it and then I'd stop worrying!

I don't think I want to ignore the problem. But how can I fight a war until I know who, or what, I'm fighting and what I can use for artillery? I've seen enough of complacent Christianity cowering in the corner of its own private apathy to the world around. In a word, I suppose I need some answers before I sink to the lowest common denominator myself! Sometimes I feel as if I'm only hanging on by my finger tips and I want to move on to a much firmer foundation.

I'm sure that you will be surprised by this—but I was really encouraged by your letter. Mankind has always had an enemy, the problem is that that enemy is an expert at camouflage. The church has found it increasingly difficult to expose his dark ways to the light of truth.

Part of our difficulty lies in the fact that Satan is a master of both lies and extremes. He hides behind both. C. S. Lewis makes a very important distinction:

> There are two equal and opposite errors into which our race can fall about devils. One is to disbelieve in their existence. The other is to believe and feel an excessive, unhealthy interest in them.
>
> Preface to *The Screwtape Letters* (Collins/Fontana, 1973)

I can imagine that your own brand of rationalism excludes too much consideration of the devil. Unfortunately his existence is not dependent upon our acceptance of it. Over the years I've seen too much of his wiles and activities to be sceptical about the existence of Satan. Tragically I've also seen many Christians becoming far too interested in the opposition and especially in demonic activities.

In part Satan's power today is the result of a lack of interest (during the first half of the twentieth century) in the supernatural aspect of Christianity. If we abdicate our commitment to a miracle-working God, then we can hardly be surprised that Satan grabs his opportunity. To this we must add the subtle fascination of the occult which has assaulted mankind ever since Eve met the serpent in the Garden.

With his own brand of devilish comprehension Satan offers two routes for people to follow.

Route 1	Route 2
'If one way don't catch you	
The other surely do.'	
Things that go bump in the night.	Fascination with the supernatural.
Scared of the dark and unknown.	Interest in ghost stories, horror comics and horror movies.

Confronting fears and finding them empty.	Research into the paranormal.
Rationalizing the unexplained.	Investigation of witchcraft and occult.
Finding the 'other reason' to explain away the supernatural.	Defying anything future to remain hidden: horoscopes etc.
Making man the ground of his own being and problems.	Dabbling in ouija boards, seances etc.
Denying heaven, hell and all absolutes.	Interest in white magic and ritual magic.
Rejecting the concept of a personal devil.	Giving reverence to the devil.

Now few people descend a long way down the slippery slope. But the problem is that whichever path is taken, or however far one goes along it, the habits of the spiritist or the sceptic are soon established. To follow to either extreme brings us into a bondage which renders us either helpless or ineffective. So Satan stalks this earth, unrecognized or blindly worshipped. Either way the spiritual ignorance which has placed him in so strong a position has made mankind vulnerable to all kinds of potent demonic stratagems.

Falling out of heaven

Satan began life as a 'Guardian cherub' who guarded the throne room of God until the day that his beauty and talents turned his head and '. . . till wickedness was found in you . . . you were filled with violence, and you sinned' (Ezekiel 28:15–16). Pride became his downfall and he was thrown out of heaven. Isaiah outlines Satan's fall in five phrases all beginning with 'I will' (Isaiah 14: 13–14).

As megalomania took control his sin progressed until finally he wanted to replace God as sovereign of the universe. Once he was expelled from heaven the earth became his battleground and our scarred earth reflects the tragic results.

The concerns expressed in your letter have been faced by Roger Price, a Bible teacher from Chichester, who wrote:

> Whether believers like it or not, and most do not, we are inevitably involved in this deadly war. Some Christians mistakenly believe that if they ignore it, or take a neutral stance, then peace will follow. Such notions can only please the devil and hinder the purposes of God. Whether we mistakenly believe we can live at peace with the devil or not, he knows that he can never live at peace with us. An attempt to be neutral is to side with the devil. A driver in a car has three choices—to go forward towards his destination, to reverse away, or to stay in neutral. . . . A believer 'in neutral' is no worry for the devil and as such frees him to devote more energy to other areas of the battle.
>
> *Victory in Jesus* (Marshalls, 1982)

Now you see why I was so pleased that you had avowed that neutrality was no position for a Christian!

Failure in the garden

One of Satan's most effective schemes is to persuade us to follow the dictates of self-interest, rather than to be obedient to God's will for our lives. Let's go back to the garden to see how Satan steadily worked out his own trap for Adam and Eve; once they broke the rules, they fell headlong into his lap!

Samuel Limbach has expressed this point very well:

> Satan is prince of this world. Faced by him man was to represent God's justice on earth. He was to rule over creation in the name of God and to work God's works within it. Thus

the enemy would be driven back legally. But if the liberation of the world was to be effected wholly according to justice and righteousness, then an opportunity had to be given Satan, God's foe, to extend his world rule of evil over man as well as being permitted to tempt him.

Quoted in E. Saver, *The King of the Earth*
(Paternoster, 1962)

This is the root of the problem and the key to the answer—if Satan is God's enemy and we are the people committed to God then he is our enemy too. So his antagonism and efforts are devoted to overturning the relationship which you and I have with the living God through his Son Jesus Christ. That is Satan's goal and objective.

Once you know what your goal is, all you need to do is to plan the right activities to achieve that goal. This quotation shows that Satan's goal was to persuade Adam and Eve to turn away from God. The best way of doing this would be to get Adam and Eve to assert themselves, instead of faithfully and obediently following God. Once that was achieved, success was assured. God and mankind would walk together no longer; the great divorce would be reality. And incredible though it may seem, both Adam and Eve made the decision to listen to Satan, despite all the advantages they enjoyed in their relationship with God.

Attack 1 (Genesis 3:1–3)

This first attack failed. Satan tried to make Eve doubt whether God had really communicated his will to her. ('Did God really say?'). Fortunately, Eve had listened carefully to God, and she had a good memory too. She was in no doubt that God had clearly revealed his will and she had taken him seriously.

The subtlety of the opening attack lay in the exaggerating of God's prohibition. By suggesting that God wouldn't allow her to eat from *any* tree, Satan tried to create in her mind the impression that God was unreasonably harsh, illogical and legalistic. Fortunately, Eve remembered that it was only the *one* tree which was out of bounds. Indeed, such was her fear of that particular tree, that she wouldn't even contemplate touching it, let alone eating from it.

Attacks 2 and 3 (Genesis 3:4–5)

Having failed to make Eve think that her ears weren't working properly, and having tried to make out that God was some kind of ogre, Satan continued to blacken God's character. His next statement, 'You will not surely die', suggested that God's threat of death was an empty one. So began the age old lie that in spite of what he had threatened, God's holiness was flexible and sin carried no penalty. Next Satan sought to implant in Eve's mind the thought that God was being mean by preventing her knowing as much as he did. Satan wanted her to believe that God was robbing them of something good, rather than acting in their best interests. In other words, he was saying, 'If God really loved you, he would let you be as wise as he is. He would tell you everything there is to know about good and evil instead of deliberately keeping you in ignorance. What an unfair God!' We must not forget that Satan himself originally fell through pride and he was aware of the power of this particular temptation to be like God himself.

Attacks 4 and 5 (Genesis 3:6–7)

Now that Eve was well on the way to defeat, Satan added his finishing touches. He made his proposition even more attractive by appealing to her taste buds and eyes. Not only did that forbidden fruit look 'pleasing to the eye' but it seemed mouth-wateringly delicious— 'good for food'. What had been just some ordinary look-

ing fruit a few minutes earlier had now become irresist-
ibly attractive as she turned it over and over again in her
imagination. The moment came when she allowed her
will to give in to her desires. With disastrous consequences.

Satan's trap had been sprung. Adam and Eve lost both
the comfort of the garden and the intimate closeness of
the relationship with God. Now sin, hostility and pain
entered their world to reign until another man came to
resist temptation and sin.

Satan's ploy had been an obvious one. Go for the
present. Take what is offered. Do your own thing. What
makes you so certain that God means what he says? But
when the consequences have to be faced, suddenly Satan
is not around any more.

Fooling himself on earth

The enemy's strategy had therefore begun well. Soon he
began counterfeiting the miraculous works of God in his
campaign to deceive mankind.

His character and activities are laid bare by the names
which the Bible employs for him:

> The accuser of the brethren (Revelation 12:10, AV)
> that ancient serpent (Revelation 12:9)
> Abaddon and Apollyon (Revelation 9:10–11)
> Beelzebub (Mark 3:22)
> Belial (2 Corinthians 6:15)
> the devil (Matthew 4:1)
> dragon (Revelation 12:9)
> the evil one (John 17:15 and 1 John 5:18)
> who leads the whole world astray (Revelation 12:9)
> a liar (John 8:44)
> the father of lies (John 8:44)
> the god of this world (2 Corinthians 4:4 AV)
> a murderer (John 8:44)

the prince of demons (Mark 3:22)
the prince of the power of the air (Ephesians 2:2 AV)
the prince of this world (John 12:31)
Satan (Matthew 4:10)
the tempter (1 Thessalonians 3:5)

These names reveal the basic problem with Satan. He is the father of lies, the arch-deceiver, and he loves acting as 'the accuser'. But his fate has been predetermined. 'The accuser of our brothers, who accuses them before our God day and night, has been hurled down.' What is more, our victory is guaranteed. 'They overcame him by the blood of the Lamb' (Revelation 12:10–11).

The name 'devil' is the Greek word *diabolos* coming from a word meaning 'to divide', 'set at variance', 'accuse', 'slander', 'reject', 'misrepresent', or 'deceive'. How many problems among Christians actually come from their failure to recognize an enemy at work among them?

However, Satan's lying character led to the inevitable denouement. Two thousand years ago he witnessed a man walking this earth in the power of God the Holy Spirit. Frankly, he panicked. At Satan's request this man was crucified but Satan failed to realize that all he was actually accomplishing was God's own loving purpose to rescue mankind from his clutches.

While Satan rubbed his hands in delight at this apparent defeat of God's Son, in the darkness of death Jesus was taking possession of the keys of Hades, releasing the prisoners, conquering the grave and rising from death into life!

Before Satan knew where he was, that one person living in the power of the Holy Spirit had ascended into heaven and there were one hundred and twenty living under the authority of the Spirit! Then there were three thousand, five thousand, and on into millions! His had been the miscalculation of eternity and Satan knew the bitter reality of total defeat.

The problem was that though defeated, Satan still wouldn't lie down. Now that he couldn't win in head-on conflict, he descended to more subtle means.

Every time, bar twice, in the New Testament the Greek word for Satan is better translated 'accuser' rather than 'opponent'. And when we stand in the authority of Christ's name, living under his blood, Satan can no more stand against us than we could stop a train at full-speed by standing in front of it. So by sly innuendo, Satan does his slippery work of spreading doubt and undermining our faith so that we fail to attain our true perfection in God.

Fulfilling God's plan—time and again

Satan's aim is always to bring about evil rather than good. He fights to reduce Christians to depths of defeat, discouragement and self-condemnation. He has a variety of methods with which he seeks to transform ordinary people into putty in his hand.

Some satanic attacks are direct and obvious but others are so subtle that we fail to notice them until it is too late. He is a master of deception and disguise. Satan may wage open warfare against us like a roaring lion, or quietly tempt us by masquerading as an angel of light. These two sides of his character are clearly illustrated in the last book of the Bible. In chapter 12, Satan is seen as a mighty fighting dragon; but in chapter 17:3–5 he resembles a seductive prostitute.

Paul describes Satan as an archer, who fires flaming arrows. These arrows of fire are carefully aimed at us! Such violent onslaughts are designed to leave Christians spiritually and emotionally wounded so that they will be in no fit state to give service and worship to the living God.

The Tempter can be so well disguised that his subtle schemes can persuade people to do the wrong thing for the best of reasons. Were they then to be told Satan had been behind it all they would be utterly amazed. Once upon a time 'the devil made me do it' was an easy escape route. But it's not a popular one today. Few recognize his subtle hand at work. There are no visible pitch-covered arrows here, but the results are equally devastating.

Take for example Satan's prime manoeuvre against a committed, growing Christian.

'You want to be careful,' he whispers, 'you can take it all too far. After all, if people sitting next to you in church knew what you'd really been like they'd move two seats away from you. What makes you think God would want to use someone like you?' Sounds familiar doesn't it?

It all sounds thoroughly frightening until we recognize two factors.

1. If Satan never challenges or attacks you then it really is only because you're not worth bothering about. If he aims his arrows at you, be glad, because obviously God is at work in and through your life.

2. Jesus never lets go of us and he is not engaging in a fifteen round boxing match with Satan. He knocked him out at the start of round one!

So when Satan attacks we must confidently take hold of the authority of the Bible as God's word, and the Holy Spirit as God's power, and then tell him to 'Get lost in Jesus' name'. When we do this he has no option but to do as he's told.

Time and again Satan over-reaches himself. Instead of undermining or destroying God's people he is allowed to test them in order that they may emerge better qualified and equipped for spiritual service.

Take Joseph, for example. Sold as a slave by his own

brothers he ended up in the household of a senior Egyptian official yet he refused to compromise his integrity. 'Joseph was well-built and handsome, and after a while his master's wife took notice of Joseph and said, "Come to bed with me!" But he refused' (Genesis 39:6–8). He was thrown into prison on a trumped-up charge but all his sufferings were only in order that he might rise to the highest position in the land, and that God's purposes for him might be totally fulfilled.

In 1984 some television programmes were shown that were clearly designed to discredit Christianity. The only obvious results were that many more people began asking questions about the nature and character of the real Jesus. Time and again Satan only succeeds in over-reaching himself, so that his efforts become counter-productive.

There is a word of warning which I need to stress to you, Harry. It's summed up in an easy phrase: *Don't count your chickens!*

'Jesus, victor over all' is one of the earliest credal statements of the church. But it's not sufficient to concentrate on this great truth alone. We are in for a dangerous time if we don't at the same time continually recognize that we are fallen beings. Our sinful human nature is an unfortunate reality.

Therefore, while Jesus always triumphs and we can enjoy the same victory if we keep our eyes fixed on him, we must never try to live in our own strength. Once that happens, before we know where we are we are starting to sink—particularly when we turn our eyes away from Jesus and look at the circumstances which surround us.

I'd like to continue on this theme because it is so fundamental to the way in which we view our Christian lives. I would appreciate it if you could be specific about areas where you 'itch' then I'll try to convey a substantial 'scratch' in the next treatise! Meanwhile, it is important to be warned about the ways in which Satan will try to cause you to take your eyes off Jesus and focus on yourself instead.

(a) *Deception*—false ideas and concepts are promulgated by Satan (1 Timothy 4:1). He is the deceiver of nations (Revelation 12:9, AV 20:3, 8, AV). He makes wrong accusations so that Christians fall into self-condemnation and therefore lead defeated lives (Job 1:6–11; Zechariah 3:1–2).

(b) *Seduction*—Satan's attacks continue by encouraging us to take our eyes off Jesus and on to his own alternatives. John summed these up as 'The cravings of sinful man, the lust of his eyes and the boasting of what he has and does' (1 John 2:16). Satan works overtime to keep Christians away from God's word. When it's time to read the Bible he makes the television, or a book, or even work seem more important.

(c) *Depression*—he causes Christians to fear everything other than God. He particularly fosters worry and unbelief—worry, instead of trust, about possessions, about death, about worldly things (1 Peter 5:7–9). And he makes believers feel tired and hopeless at prayer times.

(d) *Diversions*—he always tries to get Christians immersed into anything other than their work and witness for the Lord. As Roger Price has said,

> Satan attempts to get the believer in the wrong place (1 Thessalonians 2:18); doing the wrong things (Galatians 5:7) or thinking and believing wrong doctrine (1 Timothy 4:1 and Ephesians 4:14). Part of this is the devil's attempt to get believers preoccupied with him rather than with the Lord.
> *Victory in Jesus* (Marshalls, 1982)

Those are the dangers, but the answers are equally straightforward. Peter and Paul encourage the young Christian churches to 'Stand firm' (1 Corinthians 15:58);

'Prepare your minds for action' (1 Peter 1:13) and 'Be strong in the Lord' (Ephesians 6:10).

Follow those instructions—and keep going!

4

Who Needs Weapons Anyway?

*It was an amazing sight. The Albert Hall was full of
people. Thousands had come and it wasn't to a concert
either. On a Saturday night they had arrived for a three
hour prayer meeting.*

*I was staggered by all those people just determined to
pray for the capital city. I wish you could have seen it. I
found it fascinating—simultaneous prayer, group prayer, silent prayer, responsive prayer—there was a real
variety of prayer and it just seemed to awaken in me a
real desire to pray. Not just to mouth the words but to
discover the reality and power which lie behind them.*

*I'm afraid that your last set of comments made me
feel really inadequate.*

*I know that if I'm ever to face up to that kind of
opposition I need to find strength and resources which I
don't have. What's more, I need to be honest with you
and confess that I do find it almost impossible to pray.
Somehow there never are enough hours in the day, I
have all the right intentions, but never quite get round to
living up to them.*

*But going to that prayer meeting and sensing the
power and reality of it all just made me see sense. I
really want to get my act together as a Christian.*

I just don't believe that knowing what Jesus has already done for me is sufficient. I need to start appropriating it for myself. If I need spiritual weapons to take on enemy spirits then I want to find out where to start. It was in that large meeting that I sensed a dimension to the warfare which I had not even begun to understand. It was as if war on earth was being waged by heavenly forces, and we were right in the middle of the conflict. Not vulnerable, but protected by the Lord and taking up weapons on his behalf.

I know you've told me time and again that prayer is the key to it all. That communication with God through the direct line which Jesus has established is the most precious privilege which the Christian possesses. Well, I think I'm getting hold of that part of the picture but it's just very difficult to put it into practice.

The fact is that I've only been praying when I've been able to. Sometimes the day is just so full that there's no opportunity to get alone. Other times I find that my attempts to pray just don't seem to be getting anywhere —it's as if the telephone lines are down and I'm just not communicating. Don't get me wrong, I know that God is there, it's just that I'm not sure if I'm actually getting through!

I'm sorry to start at comic book level but it reminds me of: 'Flash, I love you—but we've only got fourteen hours to save the world!'

And so our hero rides off into the sunset to defeat the enemy with his bare hands! It almost seems unjust for our fictional super-heroes to be too well armed. After all, they have every advantage; they are certain to be victorious—the next episode, book, comic, or film depends on it!

That same sense of inevitability pervades our attitude to spiritual warfare. The living God is with us—how can we lose? So we lay down our weapons expecting to triumph, only to be defeated without even a shot fired in anger! No wonder you feel frustrated, it's more than understandable—but that's the situation we land ourselves in if we reject a regular time alone with God each day. Paul reminds us to, 'Take the helmet of salvation and the sword of the Spirit, which is the word of God. And pray in the Spirit on all occasions with all kinds of prayers and requests. With this in mind, be alert and always keep on praying for all the saints' (Ephesians 6:17–18). So how can we lay our weapons down when God has clearly called us to pick them up?

In defence of the Quiet Time

It may seem strange that the 'Quiet Time' should need defending at all! Yet today vast numbers of committed Christians view this practice with mixed feelings.

Some Christians give the idea of a daily time alone with God a very low priority. Others have gone one step further and abandoned it altogether, either for practical (I'm too busy) or for theological reasons. The latter argument claims that the whole system of Quiet Times is far too legalistic. Some maintain that a rigid discipline inhibits their enjoyment of time alone with God. They say that they can enjoy the presence of God all day long, without needing to put aside a specific time for prayer and meditation.

Now God is a loving Father who has not made us all the same. There are undoubtedly those who benefit from the release of constraint and gain a close relationship with God. However, liberty can very easily turn into licence. Most of us need basic disciplines. Without them we quickly discover that we have thrown out the baby (prayer and Bible study) with the bath water (Quiet Times).

In the early 1970s I added my voice to those who spoke of being released from the bondage of the Quiet Time and began to rely solely on the inner working of the Spirit for teaching, guidance and growth. I soon discovered that, far from developing, I was beginning to suffer from spiritual malnutrition.

I also found that it is much easier to sacrifice a spiritual discipline than to regain it!

I want to be old-fashioned and insist on a good, solid, daily devotional time. It is true that God does give us the presence of his Spirit to be with us every moment of the day. We also absorb God's word through sermons, tear-off calendars, magazines, books, etc. However, these can never be more than additional bonuses; they must never replace daily prayer and meditation on the Bible.

'Surely,' you may object, 'Jesus never had a Quiet Time?'

But then what was he doing spending so much time alone, talking with his Father, while his disciples slept, if he wasn't having a Quiet Time? (See for example Luke 4:42; 5:16; 6:12; 9:18; 11:1; 22:41.)

Korea is a nation which, in the latter half of the twentieth century, has received a touch from God the like of which has rarely been seen in the history of the church. Many denominations claim that their largest church membership is in Korea. Christian meetings have attracted attendances of over a million people. The largest individual church in the world is located in Seoul, Korea. Yet no methodology or pattern has emerged to account for such phenomenal growth.

Recently, one Korean pastor gave a clue. He spoke of the way in which nights of prayer, and prayer mountains where prayer is continually offered all day long, and every day prayer meetings at five a.m., have succeeded in dispersing armies of demon spirits leaving free ground for the people of God to occupy. Satan is not omnipresent. He can only be in one place at a time. Consequently he employs armies of demon spirits located in specific areas. In contrast Jesus inhabits the lives of each of his people by his Spirit. His power is therefore available to us and must be employed in consistent and persistent prayer if we want to regain the spiritual initiative in our land.

You mentioned how hard you find it, but perseverance establishes godly habits, and once we've gained that ground it's not so easily lost.

Waiting for instructions

Along with so many others, my first memories of prayer are a few recited words on my knees by my bed at around five years of age. However, another memory intrudes from that same era.

As, I am told, a not very sweet and innocent, but somewhat precocious six year old, I was given some verses to recite at the Sunday School anniversary. I stood there in my grey jacket and short trousers in a little village chapel and proclaimed:

> I often say my prayers,
> But do I ever pray?
> And does the meaning of my heart,
> Go in the words I say.
>
> I may as well kneel down
> And worship gods of stone;
> As offer to the living God
> A prayer of words alone.
>
> For words without the heart
> The Lord will never hear;
> Nor will he to those lips attend
> Whose thoughts are not sincere.

Talk about 'out of the mouths of babes and sucklings!'

Those words remain as true today as they were then.

Some Christians seem to believe that, having experienced a very real impetus from the Holy Spirit in their lives, a daily, disciplined prayer life is no longer such a high priority. Others regard prayer as important, but only because it salves their consciences; they feel less guilty once they've prayed. Either view is a recipe for disaster because the value and meaning of prayer has been seriously misunderstood.

Essentially, prayer is a two-way conversation between God and ourselves. We talk to him, and he talks to us. Prayer enables us to get to know God, and as our relationship develops he adjusts our direction of thought so that we begin to see things from his perspective. As we pray and study God's word, we begin to discern the heart and will of God. We then have the choice of obedience or rebellion.

For many, prayer has been so devalued that it has become merely a presentation to God of our own spiritual shopping list, a register of all those things which we long for him to do in us, or for us. We like to present the living God with our own agenda of those things which we feel he could, or should do, and ask him to bless us as we seek to perform them on his behalf.

That is not what God requires.

Often we ask God for something but appear to get no answer. James says that the lack of provision is caused by our failure to make specific requests, or because we ask for the wrong reasons (James 4:2–3).

Worth listening to

If talking to God presents problems, listening to him is even more difficult. Sometimes he wants to rebuke or challenge us, at other times he wants to bring hidden faults or potentially dangerous temptations to the sur-

face. On many occasions he simply wants us to stop talking and pay attention to him.

Some years ago Buddy Holly recorded a song called
simply 'Listen to me'. He would undoubtedly have been
surprised to know that he was using God's words to
Isaiah, 'Listen to me and do what I say, and you will
enjoy the best food of all. Listen now, my people, and
come to me; come to me and you will have life' (Isaiah
55:2–3, GNB). Each day God would have us share our
hearts with him, voicing both our concerns and desires
openly to him, then stopping in silence that he may
speak to our hearts, to direct our lives, and instruct us
about his will and way for us. Taking this opportunity at
the beginning of the day, turning ourselves over once
again to him, enabling him to set our course for the
day—doing this can truly revolutionize our lives.

Genuine prayer cannot be turned on and off like a tap.
'Your iniquities have separated you from your God'
(Isaiah 59:2). The road back comes when we count the
cost and turn to God for restoration and forgiveness.
Our hidden sins and stubborn wills have to be dealt with
before God will listen; and then we will realize that God
will not fall in with *our* way for our lives, but we must
comply with *his*! 'I know, O Lord, that a man's life is not
his own; it is not for man to direct his steps. Correct me,
Lord' (Jeremiah 10:23–24). If we don't learn to listen to
God, we could end up running our lives according to our
own human understanding, and that is a recipe for disaster! As we listen to God, and freely submit to his will,
he will tell us all we need to know. Then, when we are
asked, 'What is it you want?' (Nehemiah 2:4) as the king
asked Nehemiah, we can confidently respond with God's
will rather than just our good ideas.

Such familiarity with the will of God comes only
through the practice of being in his presence. It may
sound legalistic but I am convinced that we do need to be

disciplined in order to pray with maximum effectiveness. This is because very few feel a genuine enthusiasm for prayer day after day. For most of us it requires self-discipline to fulfil the burden of God's heart that we should be a praying people. The results can be the first steps to a much closer relationship with him.

We may also need to copy Jesus' example by fasting in order to get into the right spiritual state for communion with God. There's no standing still where prayer is concerned. We either find ourselves in a victorious, or a vicious, circle. The more we pray, the greater the ability to pray more next time. The less we pray, the less we will want to.

Help from heaven

In prayer, as in all areas of our Christian lives, there is a subtle balance between human effort and divine help. In Luke 10:38–40, Martha suggests to Jesus that she could use Mary's help. The same word is used of the assistance of the Holy Spirit for us. 'In the same way, the Spirit helps us in our weakness. We do not know what we ought to pray, but the Spirit himself intercedes for us with groans that words cannot express' (Romans 8:26). In other words when you feel that you just aren't getting through, then there is divine help at hand.

Often the reality of a situation is only exposed when we stop still and begin to consider Jesus. Meditating on him is often an essential prerequisite to seeking his will for our lives.

Ever since the Beatles latched on to Transcendental Meditation, it has become popular to examine navels, sing matras or open minds to whatever's going! Christians have, rightly, rejected these confused and dangerous practices but tragically we have also reacted against the real thing.

Every Christian has the potential to really grow in God outside of special periods set aside for personal devotion. Take a phrase from Scripture during your time alone with God and then chew it over throughout the day. Take a phrase like 'My lover is mine and I am his' (Song of Songs 2:16) or 'Peter answered, "You are the Christ"' (Mark 8:29). You'll never extract everything that God wants to reveal to you from phrases like those in an instant. So take your time. Roll them around your mind—at work, on the bus, while you're washing up. Meditate on God's great promises and discover that uncontrolled thought patterns are mastered by the word of God.

In the same way we can discover God's will only by talking to him throughout the day. Since revelation must precede intercession (in other words 'finding God's heart before seeking his face') we need to spend time with him. Waiting on God means just what it says: taking time to listen to him. The more we get to know him the easier it will be to interpret the gentle promptings of his Spirit.

Because we're so used to talking on and on, conditioned by our everyday conversations, we have failed to properly develop the art of listening—even to God! Unless we stop from time to time during the day to quietly worship him and listen to his voice it will be useless trying to bombard him with a torrent of requests.

There are times when we run out of words and God must contribute his own vocabulary. There are times when all we can do is groan inside without having a conscious knowledge of what to pray about. The Spirit joins us in this inner struggle and God interprets that joint groaning.

You see, as Sadhu Sundar Singh puts it: 'Prayer is communion with God. It is not asking God for things; it is opening our hearts to him, it is asking God for himself

(Romans 8:26–27).'

Paul urges the Ephesian Christians to 'understand what the Lord's will is' (Ephesians 5:17). In Jeremiah's day, God made a covenant with Israel: 'I will put my law in their minds and write it on their hearts' (Jeremiah 31:33). He does the same today. Through the indwelling Spirit who understands our weakness and inability to know what to pray for, God makes known his will.

Keep on keeping on

Persistence in prayer and in seeking God's will and way for our lives is absolutely essential. 'We have not stopped praying for you and asking God to fill you with the knowledge of his will' (Colossians 1:9).

Once we have received the burden of what God wants to do, our task is to get on with the job of praying. Some people suggest that you should only pray once about something and then leave the matter in God's hands. Others feel that the request should be made time and time again until God answers. Who is right? Probably both—it just depends on the circumstances.

We obviously can't pray intensively and deeply about everything. After all there are only twenty-four hours in the day. But for the bigger and more knotty issues the extent and speed with which God answers prayer does appear to be related to the seriousness and persistence with which we pray. It's not a bargain arrangement with God, but it does seem that God's answers appear to be more positive when he sees that we are deeply concerned about a matter. Jesus prayed all night long before he chose his disciples.

'But,' you may ask, 'couldn't God have told him after just one straightforward request?' Yes, of course he could, but God loves our spending time with him, and appreciates our concern to know his will.

Mark 9:29 shows that when the disciples could not cast out an evil spirit Jesus viewed their inability as due to the fact that they had not prayed sufficiently! And twice in Luke's Gospel, Jesus showed that persistence in prayer does result in receiving what we request.

In Luke 11:5–8, the story of the insistent friend needing bread at midnight illustrates the fact that God will answer the prayer of Christians who won't give up easily. He goes on to add (verses 9–10) that those who persist in asking, seeking and knocking will get their reward because God really does want to give the best to his children.

Such persistence in prayer should be a challenge to all of us. A few years ago I was around and available when a clergyman and his wife were involved in a time of real spiritual struggle. It is one of God's miracles that he uses us all to help each other. The problem is that we tend to develop quite a superior attitude to those whom God has used us to help and I was no exception. Imagine the way my pride was shattered when, a few years later, I met the clergyman and his wife again. He said to me, 'My wife and I are still so grateful for the way God used you. A day has not passed when we have not prayed for you and the family.' It is one thing to be available for a moment. It is quite another to be consistent and persistent in prayer over the years.

The same point is made by Jesus in Luke 18. A hard-hearted judge was beseiged by a widow. For a long time he ignored her but in the end he relented and responded to her pleas for justice. The purpose of the parable was not to show that God is reluctant to say 'Yes' but, 'Jesus told his disciples a parable to show them that they should always pray and not give up' (Luke 18:1).

For what kind of request is such costly, persistent prayer appropriate? Attacks of the enemy are not easy to ward off. Those praying for healing often have to struggle in prayer, and deliverance ministry can be a wearing battle. Deep-seated personal or relationship problems don't usually disappear with a single quick prayer. Important decisions can sometimes only be made after periods of heart-searching communion with God.

The Principal of Moorlands Bible College tells this story:

> At college some years ago, we borrowed money to complete a building. Someone suggested that we should pray that the whole debt would be paid off by the summer. Well, it wasn't. God hadn't answered our prayer. Why? It was because *we* had taken the initiative for setting the date rather than God. Two years later we had built a further extension and by September we owed £60,000. We asked God how he wanted us to pray. He revealed that we should ask him to be debt-free by Christmas (just 13 weeks away). As the weeks went by, the money came in steadily, so that by December 22 we only needed £15,000. But who would donate so much at that time of year? We opened the post eagerly but fearfully that week. Out fell a cheque for £10,000, then another of £4,000 and finally on the 23 December there was a £1,000 cheque. God had answered because we had let him take the initiative. When that happens eventual victory is totally assured!

Silence is golden

Four thousand people were crammed into the Big Top. But no one spoke. A little man had encouraged them to listen, to be quiet before God and no one moved. In the silence God spoke. To some all that happened was a burst of rain on the roof of the tent. Others had heard the confirmation of blessing long-promised. Apart from those few seconds there was no other rain that day. To hear that one brief downpour first required silence.

We can be too casual. Too comfortable in prayer. 'We may be striving for honesty, openness, a break from ritual, stereotype and so on, all of which are good. Conversational prayer, for instance, can be a breakthrough for some people. But because we are human, we are tone deaf to awe.' So says John White in his book *People in Prayer* (IVP, 1977) and he is right.

There comes a time when we must recognize who God is and what his character is like. He is majestic and holy. Before his glory we stay silent—and listen—in the stillness—to him.

Three thousand years ago an old priest realized that God was speaking to his young apprentice. His advice is as relevant to us today as it was all those years ago.

> Then Eli realised that the Lord was calling the boy. So Eli told Samuel, 'Go and lie down, and if he calls you, say, "Speak, Lord, for your servant is listening."' So Samuel went and lay down in his place.
> The Lord came and stood there, calling as at the other times, 'Samuel, Samuel!'
> Then Samuel said, 'Speak, for your servant is listening.'
> (1 Samuel 3:8–10)

At last God had the boy's ear. Now he could announce what he was about to do. Now Samuel was listening, he could receive his instructions. I'm not surprised that you've found it hard. Satan knows that if he can prevent an active prayer life then he's won half the battle. The strategy now must be to turn the tables on him.

5

Always a Winner!

Now that I can recognize the quality of the opposition I'm faced with a dilemma. Satanic forces could never be a walkover for a sinful man. I've never been someone who wanted to back down in the face of a problem or a crisis. I can see myself trying to fight this one alone and I suspect that it's a battle where we could never end up victorious if left to our own resources.

If that's true then I don't really understand what the preacher was getting at last Sunday. He had warmed to his theme: nothing too complicated, a simple message delivered in familiar tones. 'Are you full of problems, mortgage payments, difficulties in relationships at home or at work? You need Jesus. He is calling you tonight. Patiently waiting at the door of your heart. Why not open the door and let him in? You know that you have no answers yourself, you've tried to change things and failed. Now could be your time. How long will you reject his offer of love, joy, peace, satisfaction, fulfil- ment and happiness? Come to Jesus and your problems will be over!'

I could hardly believe my ears. My problems didn't end when I became a Christian, in many senses that's when more began! I'm not denying the reality of God's life in mine, nor the incredible difference that he is making as he works in my life. Above all, I'm not alone any more. But Jesus is not living inside me only as a friend and Saviour. He makes demands on my life as Lord and King. Often those demands are diametrically opposed to the direction in which I would want to go if I was left to my own devices. The conflict is sharp—his way or mine? But that is what I understand Christianity to be all about. The Lord of glory, the living God, is hardly going to be content with being the elixir to all my sorrows and problems while he calmly limits himself to doing what I tell him!

My understanding lies in Jesus' words, 'If any man would come after me, let him deny himself and take up his cross and follow me' (Matthew 16:24, RSV). The glib easy-believism that I was listening to must have made Satan chuckle. If ever a call to enlistment was going to enrol civilians rather than soldiers it was that one!

A speaker like that must be guaranteed to produce more spiritual still-births than healthy, growing baby-Christians. It sickened me to see the preacher reduced to the level of a door-to-door salesman of ready-packaged, bargain offer religion. Such a person was trying by slick-selling techniques, to convince any number of folk to receive 'new birth' as if God was after decisions which lasted a moment rather than disciples for a lifetime.

Hang on, I'm almost preaching! But I'm sure you've caught on to the problems. I don't believe, with the quality of spiritual opposition that we're faced with, that I can sit back as a spectator and watch it happen. If Christianity is a costly business how do I begin paying the price? I want to play my part.

So I wondered if you could work through some comments—perhaps focus on a character in the history of the church who actually took Satan on in the field of battle. I'm really quite enthusiastic to get involved—cer-

tainly the wishy-washy, pseudo-Christianity of so many holds no appeal. I want to find the real thing, but I do realize that I can't go at this like a bull in the china shop—nor can I just begin and learn as I go—I need guidelines.

Also, I'd like to know the end result. What's more, I need to see how this relates to the real world in which we live. I've been fascinated to see evangelical Christian societies getting involved and confronting councils, government and the media. The preacher I referred to reminded me of a rigid conservatism, yet other Christians seem to be challenging the status quo where it runs counter to Christian principles.

How much is the Christian life purely an individual affair, or how much should I get involved in trying to impose Christian views on a secular society?

That's a fair package of questions! The fairest answers are drawn from the life of Jesus. But let's start at Wimbledon. Forty-fifteen. Two match points. One more serve down the line, and it's all over. But it's a strain to the end, to the very last shot.

If a world class tennis player is to be successful, he must do three things. He must (1) want to be a winner above all else in life. He must (2) train relentlessly, day in and day out, never letting up the pressure. Yet although he will have benefited enormously from his determination and training, he will still need to (3) strain every muscle in each match he plays.

Strange as it may seem, Jesus was very much like this. He had only one aim in view—to please his Father. Whatever that involved in terms of personal cost, or deflecting the enemy, Jesus went through with it. The requirements of the sporting world parallel his own preparation as he fulfilled all that was necessary to make him champion of champions: King of kings!

What better object lesson could we have?

1. Singlemindedness

All his life Jesus submitted his will to one person alone
—his Father God. In fact his life revealed a totally new
dimension to devotion. His willingness to fulfil God's
every wish for his life was total and complete. He himself
said, 'I do *exactly* what my Father has commanded me'
(John 14:31). No task given to him by God was left
undone or done shoddily (John 17:4). His real hunger in
life was not for food but his Father's will. 'My food is to
do the will of him who sent me'; 'I always do what
pleases him' (John 4:34, 8:29). In his service Jesus was
not prepared to be influenced or taught by anyone except God. As an apprentice would concentrate on learning from a master craftsman, so he carefully observed
his Father's actions, learnt from them, and put them into
practice in his own life (John 5:19). His lips would only
utter that which had been taught and authorized to say
from heaven. 'I gave them the words you gave me' (John
17:8).

Faced with such a single-minded individual Satan was
utterly baffled. Jesus refused to listen to any voice other
than that of his Father God. 'I do nothing on my own
but speak just what the Father has taught me' (John
8:28). Satan would use anyone to try to deflect Jesus
from his purpose, but when a trusted disciple became the
unwitting tool of Satan, Jesus was quick to discern the
fact and rebuked Peter. 'Out of my sight, Satan!' he said.
'You do not have in mind the things of God, but the
things of men' (Mark 8:33).

All human ingenuity was rejected by Jesus; his only
wisdom came from God; any other suggestion was refused.
Such singlemindedness, such openness to the voice of
God alone, must be patiently cultivated by each one of

us in order that we, too, might live the life of our Lord Jesus here on the earth.

2. Training

Back to tennis. In January 1983 the world was shocked by the sudden retirement of Bjorn Borg, five times Wimbledon champion. Having taken a break from the pressures of top level tennis for a while in 1982, his daily hours of gruelling training became steadily fewer. By the end of the year he could no longer face the required discipline and hardship, which was so vital to get him back to the top. Later, an attempted come-back floundered on his lack of practice.

Jesus' life displayed consistent preparation for battle in four major areas:

(a) *Obedience*—even in small issues. He did what he was told! He didn't simply wait until the 'important' commands were given. Seeking out God's will and being obedient to it was normal for him. It was a godly habit standing him in good stead when major crises and pressures confronted him.

(b) *Prayer*—frequently Jesus would pray all night. His remarkable prayer life made such a profound impression on his disciples that they pleaded with him to teach them the secret! He took every opportunity to be alone with his Father—but his disciples didn't find it so easy. 'Are you asleep? Could you not keep watch for one hour? Watch and pray so that you will not fall into temptation. The spirit is willing, but the body is weak' (Mark 14:37f).

(c) *Scripture*—incredible as it may seem Jesus did not live his life in the power of the second person of the Trinity, but of the third (Luke 3:22)! It was not enough that he had been filled with the Spirit from birth. He recognized that his ministry of preaching, healing and releasing (Luke 4:18–19) was dependent on the Spirit.

For him, the Spirit was an important person in his daily life—a vital source of inspiration or power. If Jesus did not attempt to live apart from the in-dwelling Spirit, then how dare we? Because of the Holy Spirit Jesus knew he would never be deserted. 'You will leave me all alone. Yet I am not alone, for my Father is with me' (John 16:32).

3. Flexibility

Jesus used no single set pattern or strategy in fighting each battle. He didn't limit himself to any one technique when temptation faced him. In each situation he used a different form of defence. In the desert he used different verses from Deuteronomy. When people tried to make him King, he fled to the hills and prayed. Peter's suggestion that he shouldn't die was resisted by harsh rebuke. At Gethsemane, he wrestled within himself as he thought about the awfulness of the cross and the temptation to evade or to avoid it. On that particular occasion he wanted the support of his friends in his lonely struggle.

4. Resistance

Throughout the Gospels we see a continuing conflict between Christ and Satan, each committed to the destruction of the other.

Of course, the work of evil forces is described in other parts of Scripture but the clearest battles took place during the earthly life of Christ. When I was a child I was taught that demonic attacks were an Eastern disease, a special phenomenon of those days. Yet special times of demonic activity always appear to coincide with a direct move of God. Many lives are wrecked by demon spirits who will motivate self-inflicted wounds in anyone they can lay their hands on. It is therefore totally unsurprising that Satan should mobilize his prime forces against Jesus himself. From the time of King Herod's massacre of the children onwards, Satan attempted either to kill Jesus, discredit him, or trick him into avoiding the cross. But he never succeeded in winning a single victory over Jesus.

Three times Satan made his insidious suggestions and three times he was rebuffed by the Son of God.

(a) *Help yourself*

—just step out of line for a moment and turn stones into bread to feed yourself. All that was demanded was that the very kind of miracle he was to perform when he fed five thousand, and then four thousand people from a handful of food, should be advanced in the timetable so he could help himself.

(b) *Hazard your life*

—Satan quotes Scripture so eloquently. He is a better theologian than any of us, yet remains the devil still. His aim was to tempt Jesus into a spectacular 'superman-style' feat which would win instant recognition. Throw yourself down and angels will catch you. That indeed is the inference of the Psalmist but Satan quoted the verse out of context. The promise only applies as we act within the will of God. Step out of it, and Satan will have achieved his aim—smashed bones on the ground below.

(c) *Halve the cost, and the pain*

—but ruin salvation! The invitation to accept power was an attractive one. First it was being offered instantly and on a grand scale. Second, to accept it would avoid the pain of the cross. Jesus' quotation of Deuteronomy 6:13 'Worship the Lord your God, and serve him only' (Matthew 4:10) came from his knowledge that to accept power by bowing to Satan was directly contrary to the fact that his Father was the only one worthy of worship. Under no circumstances would he worship Satan.

In any case it wasn't that kind of kingdom he was setting up—it would have been no better or longer-lasting than an earthly one. The only way to the hearts of men and women was by a cross. The only means of re-uniting them to Father God was through an empty tomb.

Satan still tries the same tricks today: use God's service to advance yourself; try to achieve it by half-measures; avoid pain and a cross at all costs; go the easy way. There's no new temptation under the sun!

Jesus' friends failed and betrayed him. Often they were the unwitting vehicles of temptation and pressure but time and again Jesus conquered parts of Satan's territory which had seemed to be invincible. Every time that he cast out an individual evil spirit, healed someone, performed a miracle or released someone from bondage, he showed that he had the ultimate authority over his enemy. Jesus won every battle because he was stronger than the devil. Or, as he put it himself, 'How can anyone enter a strong man's house and carry off his possessions unless he first ties up the strong man? Then he can rob his house' (Matthew 12:29).

His binding of the strong man is a perfect example of all the principles which Jesus wants to see at work in our own lives.

(a) *Strongmindedness*
—to see God's kingdom and the perfecting of his will within our own lives, whatever the cost might be.

(b) *Training*
—in obedience, prayer, scripture and the activity of the fullness of the Holy Spirit in the life of the believer, so that God in us does his own work.

(c) *Flexibility*

—so that we never try to slot the living God into our own predetermined patterns. We do what he tells us to rather than asking him to bless our own endeavours and agenda. On our part, this involves total willingness to move in whatever direction he may choose to lead us.

(d) *Resistance to Satan*

—refusing to listen to the tempter, rejecting his easy options and recognizing that there are no short-cuts to doing the will of God.

By these means Satan's ultimate defeat is guaranteed in our lives, just as it was in the life of Jesus.

'Ah, but he was different,' is our almost automatic response. We need to remind ourselves time and again that the same Holy Spirit who raised Jesus from the dead now lives and reigns in us. Time and again Satan was knocked down by Jesus during his earthly life. Finally, at a wooden cross Satan made his fatal mistake and the crucial battle was won and lost in the supreme 'once and for all' act (Hebrews 9:26) which, as we've seen already, sealed Satan's eternal destiny in hell for evermore.

It's all over now

That was the message behind the triumphant cry from Jesus, nailed on a cross, with death beckoning. The agony of complete obedience in the garden of Gethsemane, the torture of the trial and the anguish of the most vicious form of execution which mankind has ever devised, all now lay behind him. Prophecy had all been fulfilled; he hadn't even lifted a finger to save himself.

Peter beautifully summarized Jesus' mastery of the terrible temptation to fight back. Jesus knew his Father would vindicate him. Heaven's plan involved the innocent suffering. It was the only way in which God's love and justice could be reconciled, while at the same time Satan's hold on the lives of mankind could be utterly smashed. 'When they hurled their insults at him, he did not retaliate; when he suffered, he made no threats. Instead, he entrusted himself to him who judges justly' (1 Peter 2:23).

As the time of his death grew near, Jesus announced, 'Now the prince of this world will be driven out' (John 12:31). By what means? He went on to explain that his own death would accomplish it. 'When I am lifted up from the earth' (verse 32). Similarly the writer of Hebrews says, 'So that by his death he might destroy him who holds the power of death—that is, the devil' (2:14). By voluntarily laying down his life (John 10:18) he went into the enemy's territory and conquered both Satan and death itself. In the same way that a triumphant Roman general stripped his captives of their power and led them behind him in a public victory procession, so, Paul says, 'having disarmed the powers and authorities, he made a public spectacle of them, triumphing over them by the cross' (Colossians 2:15). In that one single death of his own Son God demonstrated for ever the kind of life which he wants us to live. If you and I could grasp this for ourselves, how different things would be.

Just look at Jesus' seven statements from the cross:–

(i) 'I am thirsty' (John 19:28)—physical suffering will never be far away from God's people. A comfortable life and a Christian life can never be bedfellows.

(ii) '"Dear woman, here is your son," and to the disciple, "Here is your mother"' (John 19:26-27). A life lived for others. With his dying breath Jesus was helping others to face the future rather than bemoaning his present situation.

(iii) 'My God, my God, why have you forsaken me?' (Mark 15:34)—there will be times when God will seem to be a long, long way away.

(iv) 'Father, forgive them, for they do not know what they are doing' (Luke 23:34). Ascribing the best possible motives to our most implacable opponents and forgiving them is what is expected of us.

(v) 'Today you will be with me in paradise' (Luke 23:43). In life and death Jesus drew people from hell directed lives, and gave them a new destination—heaven.

(vi) 'Father, into your hands I commit my spirit' (Luke 23:46). He rested all the hurts and pain, the life and strength in the arms of his Father.

(vii) 'It is finished' (John 19:30). A shout of triumph, because everything that his Father had given him to do was now done.

This then is the content of the crucified life. It shows us just how far we have left to go. How do we attain it? By allowing Jesus to have control of our life and recognizing as Paul did that, 'I have been crucified with Christ and I no longer live, but Christ lives in me' (Galatians 2:20).

In other words, the answers aren't easy—but they certainly represent a pathway to a lifestyle which makes Satan tremble. The confidence which we have lies in the fact that we are not pioneering the route. Jesus has been this way already: He's charted the pathway, all you and I have to do is follow the route which he pioneered.

Candle in the dark

We have been challenged by the Lord himself to be salt and light within the nation. You see, Satan does not confine his activities to 'spiritual affairs', he is at work to undermine the fabric of society, by attacking wherever the word of God has been obeyed. And he has been outstandingly successful!

Alexander Solzhenitsyn sounded the alarm bell when he warned that if you carefully boil a frog alive in gradual stages, the poor frog never even realizes that anything is going wrong.

The principle is a straightforward one. If 'progress' is gradual enough then one scarcely notices that anything is happening. I have already written some examples of the kind of insidious and devilish changes that are taking place in our society.

Standing against the tide

Open violence, racism, urban deprivation, AIDS, un-employment—on and on goes the list of issues which to-day threaten the very jugular vein at the heart of our nation.

Many Christians may think that these comments are too political. Others regard with distaste any involve-ment in social issues. 'Our mandate is a spiritual one' is the response. The reason why I am writing like this is to remind you that Jesus challenged a real world and set us within it to act as his body—imparting salt to the world and light in the darkness.

A cosy triumphalism within our own Christian fellow-ship can never be an adequate response to the pain and depravity of a hungry hurting world. The activities of men like Wilberforce and Shaftesbury, the caring concern of Tear Fund, the committed stance of groups like the London Institute for Contemporary Christianity, the Evangelical coalition for Urban Mission, and the um-brella body, the Evangelical Alliance, clearly reveal a tradition of evangelical concern. It is a tradition which needs both encouragement and reactivation by the silent majority of committed evangelicals.

Getting used to the dark

Imagine for a moment a dark, candlelit corner of an exclusive restaurant. It's too dark to read the prices on the menu! However, by the time the dessert comes round you can see fairly clearly. The problem is that we so easily get used to the dark!

Well, I've had my little preach now, but Harry, it is an issue close to my heart. We need a singleminded concern that whatever is not acceptable to the Lord must be unacceptable to us, his people. So we do need to pray for these specifics. Petitions rarely carry much weight but personal letters of negative protest and positive alternatives evoke a response from government and media alike. Similarly, voluntary activities both in the field of relief and social concern have historically achieved great things!

As John Gladwin has summed it up for us,

> It is because this is God's world, and he cared for it to the point of incarnation and crucifixion, that we are inevitably committed to work for God's justice in the face of oppression, for God's truth in the face of lies and deceits, for service in the face of the abuse of power, for love in the face of selfishness, for co-operation in the abuse of destructive antagonism and for reconciliation in the face of division and hostility.

> *God's People in God's World* (IVP, 1979)

God's life, lived through us, will never be an easy going civilian life. It will always involve us in giving ourselves to others even when our own future is hopeless. Even when God seems far away we are still involved in the ministries of forgiveness and reconciliation so that others might receive from God all that we have first discovered. Behind it all is the certainty of victory and the knowledge that as children we can rest our lives in the arms of the living God whose life was given for ours.

Before he died as a martyr in the Ecuadorian jungles a young American missionary, Jim Eliot, wrote of his life in these words. 'He is no fool who gives what he cannot keep to save what he'll never lose.'

A Christian totally, utterly and completely surrendered to Jesus can face suffering, can care for others, isn't dependent on feelings, freely forgives, draws people heavenwards, relaxes into Father and completes the job.

That is the mark of a crucified life. It was Jesus' life, and it is the life he wants to bring about in us, as his people. What is more, he's always the winner!

6

This Dangerous Doubt

Fame at last!
I've been asked to go back to the old Poly and speak to the Christian Union. I'm really looking forward to seeing old haunts. And this time I won't be sitting at the back hoping no one notices me! The problem is that they've actually asked for a particular subject and I feel singularly unqualified.

What they want is a simple, and they underlined the word 'simple', explanation of how reliable the Bible actually is. The thing is, I don't even know where to begin and wondered if you could just start me off? I find it particularly difficult as I don't find reading the Bible any easier than leading a disciplined prayer life.

I guess that a large number of questions were sparked off by the Bishop of Durham's controversial views on the Virgin Birth and the Resurrection. What's more, the Archbishop of York made it all much more serious by his support of the Bishop's freedom to speak. I've been interested to read one or two comments that you've made on the issue so I know how you feel about the sense of uncertainty and doubt which is being created. I can see also the sense of betrayal which you and others in Christian leadership must feel. What I don't really understand is how the issues are resolved, or how the areas of difficulty have developed.

I remember that last century Oscar Wilde spoke about reasonable doubt as the essential qualification for standing at the altar and said that Thomas was his favourite apostle. It looks from the outside as if things haven't changed too much.

I listened to the Bishop of Durham speaking on TV the other day. The guy has fantastic media ability but for three quarters of an hour he explained to an audience of my generation a theology without God and a morality without absolutes. A tremendous feat of logic, but utterly disastrous as far as my simple faith goes.

I feel as if pincers are throttling evangelical Christianity. Just like the Schlieffen plan all over again. (You can tell I did history rather than theology, can't you?) On the one hand, logic and intellectual argument challenge the traditional acceptance of the Bible. On the other hand, challenging Bishop David Jenkins seems to infer intolerance, lack of love and burying your head in the sand. You seem to lose both ways.

So how can one establish that the Bible is a trustworthy record? I read with amusement the following verses in the Church of England Newspaper.

Hymn for the New Bishop of Durham

Vaguely we believe, but duly,
God is three and God is one,
But we fear we're rather woolly
When it comes to God the Son.

While in general history argues
That he may have lived on earth,
We regard with deep suspicion
Stories of a virgin birth.

We believe that Christ is risen,
Even though it were absurd

To suppose the resurrection
Has historically occurred.

Though we must not put it past him,
Signs and wonders to perform,
Reason renders most unlikely
Such departures from the norm.

To these frail and rootless doctrines
Built on legend, myth and lore,
We declare complete allegiance
Now, henceforth and evermore.

I realize that these are intended to be both humorous and facetious. Yet surely these issues are crucial for Christian belief. Thousands of clergy and leaders are obviously embarrassed and clearly the thing is blown out of proportion at times. But I've read that South African Muslims are claiming that since the fourth highest ranking Bishop of the Church of England has voiced doubts that Jesus can be regarded as the Son of God, in the historically accepted sense of these words, all Christians should realize that Muslims are right and defect to the Islamic cause!

I know my reaction may be termed immature but it does seem that to hold to Biblical truth and a God who does miracles has gone sadly out of vogue.

To answer adequately those areas of enquiry would take at least two hundred pages. I'm afraid that you're going to have to be content, Harry, with a few thoughts which hopefully, as you ask, will just get you going. Do try to read that excellent book *Doubt* by Os Guinness. You'll find it really helpful. Anyway down to work, and to the question, 'But what about the Bible?'

Jesus always had a verse for the occasion. Does that mean he had simply memorized a few proof-texts which he could glibly trot out at the appropriate moment? Certainly not! Jesus recognized that to succeed in spiritual battle with Satan, even he needed to stand on the firm foundation of the Bible—the word of God.

God's word now!

Jesus was quick to ask, 'Have you never read in the Scriptures?' (Matthew 21:42); to rebuke, 'You are in error because you do not know the Scriptures' (Matthew 22:29); and to encourage, 'He explained to them what was said in all the Scriptures concerning himself' (Luke 24:27). He gave this high place to the Old Testament. The New Testament, of course, wasn't even written. Yet how many of us have never even read through the Old Testament?

Jesus criticized those who were ignorant of the Old Testament. His own personal acquaintance with Scripture provided a vivid contrast with the shallow knowledge of his opponents. When they confronted him with particular problems, Jesus had such a good grasp of the Bible that he immediately knew which part was relevant.

We each need to be similarly acquainted with the contents of the Bible, and able to apply its teaching to our lives. The many purposes outlined in 2 Timothy 3:16 can only be fulfilled in our lives if we are intimately aware of the content of God's word. As verses 16–17 state: 'All Scripture is God-breathed and is useful for teaching, rebuking, correcting and training in righteousness, so that the man of God may be thoroughly equipped for every good work.'

Just imagine for a moment your sense of embarrassment on arriving in heaven only to meet Obadiah whose first question is, 'Well, what did you think of my book?' And you've never even read it!

Paul urged the Colossian Christians to, 'Let the word of Christ dwell in you richly' (Colossians 3:16), and to be prepared to receive guidance and direction from it. This requires careful study and so takes time. A two minute whizz through a passage is inadequate if we are to engage in a serious search for what God wants us to learn from his word.

The apostle John gives us a particularly good reason for immersing ourselves in the Scriptures: 'I write to you, young men, because you are strong, and the word of God lives in you, and you have overcome the evil one' (1 John 2:14). Here he implies a vital link between a thorough knowledge of the Bible and the status of being an 'overcomer'. Those who are equipped and enriched by the Bible will be able to defeat the enemy through the spiritual strength they have gained from Scripture. And we must remember that when the Holy Spirit strikes the enemy he picks up his sword for the purpose. The Bible alone is the sword of the Spirit! What better weapon could be given us?

The other parts of the Christian armour which Paul outlined to the Ephesians were all there for defence. The Bible is God's weapon for offence, and as such we need to learn how to use it. Once you know how to employ it—then Bible and prayer become twin weapons in your Christian life.

Counter-attack

It has long been accepted that attack can be the best means of defence. At a time when Satan could be cowering in a corner covered with fear, he launches a bitter counter-attack.

The eighteenth century was a time of great evangelical revival, with major results in society. People with no interest in spiritual things woke up to Christian truths when men like John Wesley and George Whitefield preached the Bible as established fact.

A second evangelical awakening followed in the

middle of the nineteenth century as thousands of people committed their lives to Jesus Christ.

The keynote of evangelical Christianity does not lie in forms of worship or styles of church government. That is why one will find evangelicals in just about every denomination. For them, the crux of the matter is that their lives are committed to the Jesus who is revealed in Scripture and their lives are pledged to be lived in accordance with what the Bible instructs. Such a lifestyle is made possible only by the power of the Holy Spirit indwelling each person who surrenders his life to Jesus Christ.

Knowing this to be true, Satan's strategy was remarkably clever. He set out to discredit the Bible's claim to be God's unique revelation to mankind. By doing this, he could at the same time cast doubt on the reality of Jesus and destroy the basis for understanding Christian conduct and truth! Putting doubt in the mouth of contemporary ecclesiastical leaders was a potent refinement of his strategy.

Contemporary TV programmes which have purported to reveal the truth about Jesus have done no more than highlight the development of Satan's programme of resistance to evangelical arguments for the truth of Scripture.

We may be unaware of the spiritual potency of the Bible but Satan certainly does not share our ignorance! That is why during the last 150 years he has focused a greater measure of attack on the truth and value of the Bible than on any other book in world history.

The three-pronged attack has been simple in concept.

(a) *Don't believe it!*

Around the end of the nineteenth century influential theologians strongly maintained that it was no longer possible to discover the facts about Jesus. The theory is that because the Gospels speak of events which followed the Roman conquest of Jerusalem in AD 70 they must have been written later than that date. The later they were written, the less likely they were to be authentic.

But times have changed. Although there are still scholars who feel like that, most are not so gloomy. Archaeological discoveries have supported the claims of the Bible concerning the general situations it describes. Recently discovered manuscripts have made us more certain that the text is correct.

Bishop John Robinson, once the doyen of critical scholars, describes the period of time between the resurrection of Jesus and the production of the Gospels as the 'tunnel period'. At the end of this time the train emerges, laden with the baggage of ecclesiastical language.

'Obviously,' says Robinson, 'the shorter the tunnel— or period between the events and writing—the less is the likelihood of distortion.' He dates almost all the New Testament documents before 70 AD. This makes the gap between the events described and the time of writing around a mere thirty-five years.

It is interesting to note that the Roman historian Tacitus wrote what is generally accepted as an accurate history of the reigns of Tiberius to Nero from between forty-five to eighty years after the events. Yet, many theologians have asserted that the New Testament writers produced almost total distortions a mere thirty-five years after the events!

Archaeology provides some corroborative evidence. However, archaeology can only verify Biblical situations, rarely can it positively support biblical facts. No discovery has been unearthed to prove that a man named Abraham ever set out from Ur of the Chaldees in response to the call of God. What modern archaeology can do is confirm the accuracy of the biblical account of the societies in which Abraham lived.

In John 5 the description of the pool of Bethesda, with its five porches, was held by many scholars to be very fanciful and no more than a fabrication to enhance the story. However, in the early 1930s, the whole site was unearthed and excavated and found to be exactly as John had described it—complete with the five porches! At the very least we can be certain that no archaeological discovery has yet been made which disproves any section of the biblical narrative.

(b) *Don't read it*

Scripture is designed to evoke a response from us. An academic enquiry is insufficient. It has often been affirmed, 'God said it, I believe it, and that finishes it!' But does it?

The Bible writers intended that God's words should result in action. Yet all too often the best-selling book of all time is left on the shelf, unread and not acted upon.

I don't know if you've ever noticed that non-Christians are always in the vanguard of opposition to contemporary changes in the church? New translations of the Bible meet with their disapproval too. They like to respect Christianity's traditional place in the life of the nation, to have a Bible *on display* but a modern translation which would be easy to read does not fit the bill. Satan's subtle ploy to suggest that Scripture is not for reading has been incredibly effective.

People make extraordinary claims about Jesus based entirely on ignorance or misinformation, because they've never actually bothered to explore the truth. A hundred years ago, Lew Wallace, the Governor of Alabama, sat down to write a book which would explode, once and for all, the crazy claims of Jesus Christ. After four years of research he began writing, only to find that he could not go on. He no longer believed what he was writing! So he turned the book into a novel confirming his new-found belief, forced on him by the evidence, that Jesus really is the Son of God. And that, to cut a long story short, is how the world gained *Ben Hur*!

To read the Bible does not mean simply skimming through its words like those of a cheap novel. We need to take time, memorizing sections, digesting and meditating over portions, letting God actually speak to our situations through his word.

A regular, disciplined plan of reading can be a great help. I tend to try to average four chapters a day, reading in parallel one chapter from Genesis, Ezra, Matthew and Romans onwards. That way in just over a year the whole of the Old Testament is covered once and the New Testament three times. Alternatively, a vast number of Bible-reading aids are available and can be really helpful in providing a pattern for daily study.

(c) *Don't trust it!*

This last strategem has proved to be Satan's most successful lie about the Bible. His argument is that the Bible is a biased, and consequently largely untrustworthy document. It must not, therefore, be taken too literally and vast exercises of mental gymnastics are necessary to understand it. The result has been that the Bible is largely seen as complicated, boring, and open to all kinds of different interpretation, a book for the expert who can sort out good from bad, and strictly not for the innocent layman.

This argument comes from the idea that after Jesus' life on earth information about him circulated in units of tradition designed to meet the needs of the church. These units were consciously or unconsciously tampered with to answer the complaints of critics so that a 'hotch potch' of miscellaneous miracles and teaching emerged from the collective Christian imagination. Because they were compiled and selected after the first Easter it is held that they must have been made from the standpoint of commitment and must display a distinct bias.

These beliefs have permeated the minds of many who would sincerely regard themselves as enlightened Christians who are helped by their faith.

A letter to the Methodist Recorder outlines this position:

At the meeting of our Methodist Fellowship on Sunday evening Lord Soper's article protesting against campaigns conducted under the banner 'The Bible Says . . .' was read and discussed. The fellowship asked me to write and express their agreement with the article and their appreciation of the fact that Lord Soper had written it at this time.

Some members of the fellowship spoke of their own pilgrimage from fundamentalism in their youth to a more mature understanding of the Bible. At first their doubts about the literal interpretations had been accompanied by a sense of guilt, but they had eventually come through to a liberating and positive approach to the Bible which had enabled them to understand many things which had formerly seemed obscure or frankly incredible.

That same morning our minister had spoken about the feeding of the five thousand—a source of immense difficulty, if taken literally, for anyone with a scientific training. He showed us so clearly the inner meaning of this story, that in spiritual things the more we give, the more we possess, that the literal meaning no longer seemed important.

The fellowship discussed the widespread psychological need for something infallible to cling to: some Roman Catholics to the infallibility of the Pope (speaking ex cathedra), some evangelicals to the infallibility of the Bible . . . and so on.

While we were sympathetic to the psychological needs of the insecure, we hoped that Methodists would constantly be helped to grow into more mature attitudes and that our ministers would not avoid such questions for the sake of peace, but give their people the kind of lead for which we are so grateful to Lord Soper.

Whereas one would want to sympathize with the sincere and committed churchmanship which underlines such comments, they have become far too common among church leaders. Raising doubts about the veracity of the resurrection or virgin birth may appear to be scholarly, but can scarcely be helpful. Now if these doubts were more than mere speculation they could be taken seriously. But while the Gospel records might lack evidence, many of these wild theories possess none at all and can appear to be scaremongering at best!

I find it significant that Jesus used Scripture against Satan. Perhaps it is only inevitable that Satan would seek to discredit Jesus by attacking Scripture. A self-confessed 'white witch' commented recently in a letter to a friend: 'The Bible is man-made, written by scribes and prophets from all credos of life. It is a mish-mash of contradictions from start to finish.' It is startling and disturbing to note that the comments of many theologians often sound like statements from prophets of the occult.

A totally different view is presented in the careful work of Dr B. Gerhardsson. In *Memory and Manuscript* (1961), Dr Gerhardsson faced up to the fact that there was a period of time before the Gospels were produced in manuscript form when their content was passed by word of mouth, with all the potential for distortion or fabrication. But studies have shown that the oriental memory was peculiarly retentive. Many Jews knew the first five books of the Old Testament off by heart. Teaching in school was done by memory. Gerhardsson's main contention is that rabbinical teachers not only taught traditional material, but taught it in set forms and vocabulary which the pupils were expected to learn by heart.

Professor Howard Marshall of Aberdeen University writes, 'It is highly probable that what Jesus taught his disciples during his lifetime was remembered accurately, passed on and kept alive by fresh applications to new audiences.'

Minor miracles?

It is currently much in vogue, as you have pointed out, to seek to discredit all supernatural ingredients in the Biblical record. Miracles do not conform to the rationalistic standards of the modern mind. Rather than man's intellect being measured by the standards of Scripture, the reverse procedure is introduced. If we can't believe it, then we are supposed to accept that it could never have happened.

Most of the major denominations no longer demand belief in the miraculous as a tenet of belief for church membership. But the problem is that miracles are not isolated instances in Scripture. The Biblical writers scarcely viewed them as unimportant fictional adjuncts to faith. Theirs was a faith they would die for—because it worked in practice. Such confidence can be ours today as we see our God working in miraculous ways in our world. Take away the supernatural and what is left? Another philosophy, another code of rules and regulations? But where is the power of God if he is confined to working within the limitations of the mind of man?

Last year I returned from a trip to the USA to discover that my oldest son, Kristen, had broken a bone in his foot. The family was due to go on holiday to Spain the following week! Kristen was nearly able to swim and we had looked to that holiday as the time when he could learn properly. I pictured with dismay his frustration at being in bandages all fortnight.

However, I was much reassured, as you can imagine, by hearing that the Church leaders had been round to pray for him. One of them, Steve, had sensed that God was giving a simple word about the lad—'Nine days time'. Now that was the day before the holiday began and three weeks before medical science felt that he would be able to walk.

So we waited patiently for the healing. That exact day our local Christian doctor rang us up. For some reason, why he wasn't sure, he had been looking at Kristen's X-rays and had realized that instead of one broken bone there were in fact three! Instead of a bandage, Kristen now had to go to hospital for a plaster cast.

It was so easy to believe that Steve had it all wrong. Kristen went off to hospital with a friend who returned with this story.

Our little five year old son had started chatting-up one of the Ward Sisters. She had been fascinated by him and overrode protests to insist that instead of having a plaster put on he should be X-rayed again. The X-rays revealed that the bones had knit together! The next day he was walking again.

Such stories can be multiplied by the thousand as the churches in this country have recovered the truth that God still performs signs and wonders today.

The superman syndrome

The demonic and supernatural have also come under heavy attack from sceptical theologians. These have been relegated to the level of comic-book fairy tales for the innocent or gullible.

Of all the gospel writers Luke, a physician, should have had his feet firmly on the ground. He compiled an impressive casebook of evidence of supernatural activity, and also pointed out that signs and wonders serve the purposes of God at all times—in the cases of Elymas, and Ananias and Sapphira with devastating consequences.

I recently compiled a brief list for a series of seminars. If nothing else it shows that in Luke's writings alone the vindication of the good news was clearly perceived in the visible overthrow of the kingdom of darkness and the new dimension of God's power at work both in and through his people. Remove these, and there is little left of the Gospel. Perhaps one is reduced to a recent cartoon caricature of the well-known Bishop you referred to hanging on to a piece of paper for all his worth. After all, it was all that was left!

Luke Shows How the Kingdom of Darkness Is Overthrown

A. Death Denied

JESUS	HIS PEOPLE
(a) Zechariah's prophecy— Luke 1:79	(a) Satan's power reversed— Acts 5:10, 12:23
(b) The great escape— Luke 4:29-30	(b) Dorcas raised— Acts 9:40
(c) Power of death annulled— Luke 9:27	(c) Resurrection declared in Athens—Acts 17:31
(d) Eternal resurrection— Luke 20:36	(d) Idol worshippers afraid— Acts 19:27
(e) Thief in paradise— Luke 23:43	(e) Eutychus raised— Acts 20:9
(f) Glory declared— Luke 24:26	(f) Paul saved from death— Acts 28:6
(g) Jesus goes to heaven— Luke 24:51	
(h) Jesus raised by God— Acts 10:40	

B. Satan Destroyed

(a) Temptations ignored— Luke 4:1–13	(a) Authority given to the disciples—Luke 9:1
(b) Forgave sins— Luke 7:48	(b) Demons submit to the 72— Luke 10:17
(c) The kingdom has come— Luke 11:20	(c) Jesus prays for Peter— Luke 22:32
(d) The finger of God— Luke 11:20	(d) Salvation declared— Acts 2:21
(e) Son of man will come— Luke 12:40	(e) Evil spirits removed in Samaria—Acts 8:7

JESUS	HIS PEOPLE
(f) Jesus' strategy fulfilled— Luke 13:32	(f) Simon converted/ Discredited—Acts 8:11–12
(g) Righteous to rise— Luke 14:14	
(h) Jesus to rise— Luke 18:33	
(i) Coming of the Spirit— Acts 1:5	

C. Demons Defeated

(a) Demons couldn't injure in front of Jesus—Luke 4:35	(a) Elymas defeated— Acts 13:10
(b) Cast out many demons— Luke 6:18	(b) Slave girl delivered— Acts 16:18
(c) Continued that work— Luke 7:21	
(d) Delivered Legion— Luke 8:30	
(e) Exposed the demons and their influence—Luke 8:33	
(f) Restored the man— Luke 8:35–36	
(g) Jesus healed boy and taught disciples a lesson— Luke 9:42	
(h) Wandering spirits— Luke 11:24	

Why is it all so important?

Every faith has its own religious writings. Scripture claims to be the revelation of God and removes our doubt and dependence on our own thoughts. It is quite clear that society deals in shades of grey but the Bible spells God's truth out in black and white. Truth for the Christian is therefore not relative but biblical!

The name 'evangelical' has traditionally been given to

Christians who find their security in a personal relationship with Jesus Christ under the authority of the Bible as the revelation of his personality and will.

In any conflict we need weapons. It is for us to be certain that we keep them sharp and prepared for use in warfare. We need to make sure that we do not neglect Scripture but spend time in studying God's word. In that way we can put on the rest of the armour which God provides and move out confidently into battle—'Put on the full armour of God, so that when the day of evil comes, you may be able to stand your ground, and after you have done everything, to stand' (Ephesians 6:13).

The Bible gives us confidence. It is the foundation and the security on which we build. Where that is undermined, then everything else begins to totter. In a world of uncertainty the sword of the Spirit provides our weapon for offence and for defence—so don't let go!

7

Some Things We Just Don't Talk About

Why is it always when things seem to be going really well it all comes crashing down? I was so grateful that you took the time to write. I know we agreed that I would initiate the correspondence, so after months of silence it was discerning of you to break the rules. It must have been fairly obvious to you that things wouldn't always go as well as they were—however, the fall was as alarming as it was sudden.

I've always disliked any kind of 'up and down syndrome' among Christians. You know, up one moment and down the next! When it happened to me I was so surprised! Oh, I know I was keeping up a good impression, maintaining the facade and all that, but a lot of things were happening inside which I just wasn't prepared to admit to anyone—let alone myself!

It was all so subtle. I just began harking back to the old times, days I'd left behind held an attraction which I'd never noticed at the time. Then the old reactions and old desires started to return as well.

Somehow the time spent with Christians frustrated me. Fellowship wasn't scratching where I was itching! At church, everything was very orthodox but although both sermons and worship were helpful they only seem-

ed to touch the surface of all that I was feeling.

Then I started to feel lonely. There was this girl at work—and you know the rest! If that wasn't bad enough, she was married too! I didn't make love to her, something made me stop short of going that far, but just about everything else went on.

I found myself trying to rationalize it all. If it felt good and right, why wasn't it acceptable? After all the church needs to be progressive in its attitude, doesn't it?

Still, I wasn't satisfied with my own answers. My times alone with God became less and less frequent. Priorities seemed to change. Words like 'backsliding' hadn't been in my vocabulary but that certainly describes the condition that I was in.

Well, I'm in a house group at the church and so I thought I'd better talk it over with the group leader. But he wasn't much help, he told me I was wrong—but I knew that. He didn't tell me what I needed to hear, which was why things had started to go wrong. But then, as he said, no one had ever told him how to cope with these kinds of problems. However, he did say that I ought to repent. Confession, I found, was good for the soul and I gave all the mess to God with my pledge that I really did want to walk in the opposite direction.

In the middle of all this your letter arrived!

I suspect that you're not going to be too shocked, nor that the timing of your letter was an accident. However, even though the affair is over, the feelings of shame and self-disgust are very real. I don't understand why things have worked out like this. I always thought that I'd be the one who would be consistent and faithful. And yet I feel a little as though things might have been different if only I'd been warned. Still, 'If only' are easy words to use and I'm running out of excuses!

Some words create an embarrassed silence! Immediately

the atmosphere completely changes. Try talking about sin at a party, or in a bus queue. Watch for the reaction!

No one cares to admit the truth. Men and women were made to know and love the living God and instead they have chosen to do their own thing! This rejection of life lived in submission to, and in relationship with, the living God has produced the great divorce. The rebellion, as old as history itself, reveals sin as it really is: not just an action, but a whole way of living as if God does not exist. Of course, individual sinful actions are multitudinous, but they represent the symptoms rather than the cause.

Last year our local Free Church unveiled a tapestry designed by Jack, a headmaster, who is one of the church members. The local newspaper covered the story and took advantage of one phrase from the headmaster, taken out of context, to construct a whole article.

Jack had dared to say that he felt the church was proclaiming the good news of who Jesus really was, but in a sinful city. A local clergyman from the ecumenical church joined the debate declaiming that the city was no more sinful than anywhere else—so losing a golden opportunity to proclaim the release of sin offered by Jesus. It all seemed like another attempt to whitewash society and cast doubt on the mental stability of the congregation.

Jack, who had been a Christian for less than two years, was determined to redress the balance. He picked up his pen to inject truth into the debate:

> It is fashionable these days to reserve the word 'sin' to account only for extreme acts of criminal or sexual deviance.
>
> According to this definition only a very small minority of people would be classed as sinful. . . . But the word sin has its origin in the Bible, as its meaning is an act against the word of God.
>
> Milton Keynes *Mirror*, December 22, 1983

For three chapters in his epistle to the Romans, the apostle Paul wrestles with this problem until he arrives at this devastating conclusion: 'For all have sinned and fall short of the glory of God' (Romans 3:23).

I'm really grateful that you've come out into the open and been honest about all that has happened. It is sometimes easy just to dismiss our faults. What is harder is to acknowledge guilt and then rebuild on the basis of God's forgiveness. From my position, it would be easiest to murmur sympathetic noises. Instead I want to be brutally honest because sometimes sin acts as a vivid illustration of the way that there are some things we just don't talk about. If we used one quarter of the hours we spend discussing violence or nuclear devastation in quietly analysing the tragic effects of sin on our world, our perspective could be so different! Physically, our world is in danger, but spiritually it hangs on the brink of the precipice. God's word declares that our world will not disintegrate in nuclear holocaust, but will face its final curtain call at the second advent of the coming King. For that we need to be ready. Millions are attempting to live without God. We have truth to tell, and to live. Which is why we, too, must talk about sin in our own lives in order that we might truly discover a radical alternative and demonstrate to a dying world what a living God can do.

But, of course, some things we just don't talk about! In the church, too, we rarely face up to the fact of sin with the honesty that Scripture displays. Tragedy normally results.

The heart of the matter

At the heart of Satan's deceptions lies the accusation that God is not totally trustworthy. He also whispers to us that we should forget all that God has done for us in the past and simply confront the blank-faced brick wall of the present.

Joseph decided not to commit adultery with Potiphar's wife, because he recalled with gratitude the goodness of God. Despite the obvious pleasure being offered to him, he knew deep down that it would be dishonouring to God, and like any cheap bargain would turn out to be expensive in the end (Genesis 39:7–9).

King David, on the other hand, sinned against Bathsheba. As Nathan pointed out afterwards, David's sin was totally inexcusable in the light of all the fantastic things he had received from God (2 Samuel 12:7–9). If only he had thought about them at the moment of temptation!

In honesty I have to say that I wish you had followed Joseph's example rather than that of David. You were really making progress in your relationship with the Lord. The fact that you spoke to that Christian Union meeting and were working in the youth club meant that you were a threat to Satan, so he challenged you, and you failed in the test. Not the first, nor the last, but it was a tragic and stupid mistake, the consequences were inevitable, and tragic.

God does two things when we turn to him in true penitence and seek for his forgiveness. First, he freely offers a fresh start, but, second, he reminds us of his parting shot to the woman caught in the act of adultery. He freely forgives her, but adds this warning, 'Go now and leave your life of sin' (John 8:11).

A proper foundation needs to be established in all of our lives so that acts of sin mark not a precedent but a conclusion. God has promised privileges to his people but these are all contingent upon our obedience to his will and to his revealed instructions.

We must each of us answer the question, 'Am I so fully convinced of the goodness and provision of God that I'll always turn to him instead of yielding to the desire to do it for myself, in my way?' If not, we must face the reality, that would be breaking the rules, and as such is forbidden!

Who's fooling whom?

They had been married for three years. He was a respected leader in the local church. His first wife had died and left him with three boys. He married a Christian girl, and she gave him another son. They had their ups and downs like most couples—but then one day he announced that he was leaving with another man's wife; a girl who had recently been converted. They intended to set up home together.

In a parallel situation a respected Christian leader, known throughout the country, walked out on his wife and family to start again.

One thing that stands out is that both men made the same comment: 'Now I feel much closer to the Lord than I did when I was with my wife. I know I'm going on much more as a Christian.'

Scripture is quite straightforward: 'Husbands, love your wives, just as Christ loved the church and gave himself up for her to make her holy. . . . In this same way, husbands ought to love their wives as their own bodies. He who loves his wife loves himself. . . . each one of you also must love his wife as he loves himself, and the wife must respect her husband' (Ephesians 5:25–26, 28, 33). Or, more bluntly, 'You shall not commit adultery' (Exodus 20:14).

God has made rules. That is what the commandments were for. They were to be kept, and not broken, in order that God's rules for society might be maintained among his people. Those rules were not to be broken and God longs to give us his strength, love and obedience in order that 'The fear of God will be with you to keep you from sinning' (Exodus 20:20).

It's easy to try to delude ourselves, but Jesus himself pointed out if we really love him then we will do what he tells us. And that means keeping the rules!

Just won't stay lying down!

One of the greatest problems which Christians face today is the struggle for consistency. Hard as we try, our spiritual lives are more like a yo-yo, up and down, up and down, than a graph of steady progress. Any claim to being sinless we know is just nonsense, our only real hope is that we might be sinning less, and even that we're not too sure about.

In his first epistle John describes three *wrong* attitudes which we can adopt towards this subject that we all know too much about.

(a) We're not sinners at all, either by nature or by deed. 'If we claim to be without sin . . .'' (1 John 1:8).

(b) We admit to being sinners by nature but we don't commit acts of sin: 'If we claim we have not sinned . . .'' (1 John 1:10).

(c) We are sinners and commit sins but they are of little importance because they fail to prejudice our relationships with people or with God. 'If we claim to have fellowship with him yet walk in the darkness'' (1 John 1:6).

If we have committed our lives to Jesus Christ and have received his forgiveness, then we know that the first attitude cannot apply to us because we freely admit to being sinners. Our spiritual history has progressed from ignorance to recognition that our independence of spirit and lifestyle has branded us as sinners who have rejected the direction and authority of God over our lives. Consequently we realize that the second and third attitudes outlined in 1 John are also wrong. We know we've committed specific actions which have hurt both God and other people. These have formed a barrier to our enjoyment of God and therefore deserve punishment. At the same time we hear the good news that Christ died for our sins, and because of that glorious fact we are forgiven, credited for righteousness, and have direct access to a holy God.

We remain inwardly sinful. But it is a comfort to know that when we do sin it is already covered by Christ's blood. Through confession and repentence, our fellowship with God is restored. With God's help, we then try to live in a way that pleases him.

All this is true. It is, however, only part of the story about our connection with sin. It is easy to be comparatively naive about sin, but such short-sightedness leads us into miserable, fruitless, Christian lives.

If we claim that we never sin, then all we do is deceive ourselves. If we misunderstand what sin really is, then we can lull ourselves into a false sense of security by kidding ourselves that we rarely, if ever, do anything wrong. If we regard sinning as relatively unimportant, then we fail to realize the damage it causes in our relationships both with God and with his people.

This is the most important weapon in Satan's demonic armoury. By skilful use of sin Satan misled Adam by deceiving Eve, destroyed Samson, wiped out Sodom and Gomorrah and misdirected the entire human race by directing them down a one-way street to destruction, and eternal damnation. Or so he thought! God's rescue operation in the person of his Son, Jesus, was an unqualified success. Still the battle continues—Satan is now defeated but he just won't lie down!!

Committing the sin—but keeping the rules

Many have been wrongly taught that the essence of Christian living lies in strict adherence to a series of do's and don'ts! By faithfully observing all the rules, we can genuinely convince ourselves that we have virtually solved the sin problem in our lives.

This is what happened to the church at Colossae. The people in the church there were very preoccupied with spiritual-sounding laws—'Do not handle! Do not taste! Do not touch!' (Colossians 2:21). Some believed that by following these rules they could make their lives entirely pleasing to God. Similarly, we may feel that once we have been delivered from a particular list of private or public sins (e.g. immorality, lying, cheating or flying right off the handle!) then all is well. We are relatively sinless!

'So, what's wrong with that?' you may ask. The trouble is, when we think that we've finally cracked the 'sin' problem we become smug and complacent about our Christian lives while being critical of others who don't keep 'our' rules. We freely label them as worldly, carnal, or as backsliders. This was the attitude of the Pharisees in Jesus' day. In order to be quite sure that they were obeying God completely, they explained and analysed each commandment, breaking each one down into a system of minute regulations to cover every eventuality. For example, they unpacked the fourth commandment, giving their own interpretations of what it meant to keep the Sabbath day holy. Work was forbidden. So—in to-day's terms—passing a cup of tea to a guest is forbidden —but not if it is passed on the back of the hand! A parcel cannot be carried by hand—but it can be suspended from the ear and transported that way! Nothing can be tied except a belt for a lady's dress; so tying your delphiniums can be done on the Sabbath—but by the wife's belt only! Those illustrations depict a dangerously legalistic, and somewhat farcical degree of spiritual nitpicking!

We need to demonstrate an alternative attitude to obedience. Rebecca Manley Pippert tells a lovely story in this connection:

When I first came to Portland, Oregon, I met a student on one of the campuses where I worked. He was brilliant and looked like he was always pondering the esoteric. His hair was always mussy and in the entire time I knew him, I never once saw him wear a pair of shoes. Rain, sleet or snow, Bill was always barefoot. While he was attending college he had become a Christian. At this time, a well-dressed, middle-class church across the street from the campus wanted to develop more of a ministry to the students. They were not sure how to go about it, but they tried to make them feel welcome. One day Bill decided to worship there. He walked into this church, wearing his blue jeans, tee shirt and, of course, no shoes. People looked a bit uncomfortable, but no one said anything, so Bill began walking down the aisle looking for a seat. The church was quite crowded that Sunday, so as he got down to the front pew and realized that there were no seats, he just squatted on the carpet—perfectly acceptable behaviour at a college fellowship, but perhaps unnerving for a church congregation. The tension in the air became so thick one could slice it.

Suddenly an elderly man began walking down the aisle toward the boy. Was he going to scold Bill? My friends who saw him approaching said they thought, 'You can't blame him. He'd never guess Bill is a Christian. And his world is too distant from Bill's to understand. You can't blame him for what he's going to do.'

As the man kept walking slowly down the aisle, the church became utterly silent, all eyes were focussed on him, you could not hear anyone breathe. When the man reached Bill, with some difficulty he lowered himself and sat down next to him on the floor that Sunday. I was told there was not a dry eye in the congregation.

Out of the Saltshaker (IVP, 1979)

God never intended that Christianity should be a mere series of do's and don'ts. That is why Jesus was so angry with the Pharisees. The other religious party in his day was the Sadducees; they rejected much biblical teaching as untrue yet Jesus was nowhere near as hard on them as he was on the Pharisees. Why was that?

Jesus loathed and detested hypocrisy. He knew that the Pharisees were deeply concerned about trivial details which cost them little while totally ignoring basic issues which might have involved drastic changes in their life-style. 'Woe to you Pharisees, because you give God a tenth of your mint, rue and all other kinds of garden herbs, but you neglect justice and the love of God' (Luke 11:42).

Jesus talked of those who strained over gnats but swallowed camels! We do the same:

> Take a sixty year old maiden lady. Never in her life has she drunk even a glass of sherry. She has never owned a TV set. She has never—oh but *never* smoked a cigarette. She tithes religiously. Her hem lines are low and her neckline high. Her jewellery is anonymous. She attends the Wednesday night prayer meeting without fail.
>
> Yet she gossips. She is self-righteous. The rumours she spreads about the church young people are not only inaccurate but damaging. She calls the pastor almost every day with some new and juicy bit of scandal. She is a strainer at the gnats of movies, TV, and dancing, and a swallower of the camels of gossip, divisiveness, judgmentalism and unkindness. And she will always be a frustrated, unhappy woman.
>
> John White, *Flirting with the World*
> (Hodder & Stoughton 1982).

Now it may well be right to attend the prayer meeting and avoid alcohol—but sin is more than obeying the rules; it is keeping our hearts clean, clear and right before God and each other.

Those who claim that keeping man-made rules keeps them free from sin make God out 'to be a liar' (1 John 1:10). Although a watertight system of do's and don'ts appears to lead to true holiness, Paul says that the opposite occurs. The law was given as a schoolmaster to lead us to Christ; once we have surrendered to him we come into a relationship with a far higher standard of obedience.

The old rules 'are all destined to perish with use, because they are based on human commands and teachings,' says Paul. He continues, 'Such regulations indeed have an appearance of wisdom, with their self-imposed worship, their false humility and their harsh treatment of the body, but they lack any value in restraining sensual indulgence' (Colossians 2:22–23).

Does this mean we can get away with anything and everything? No way. Paul quickly reminds them that while ignoring human traditions they must—'Put to death, therefore, whatever belongs to your earthly nature: sexual immorality, impurity, lust, evil desires and greed, which is idolatry' (Colossians 3:5).

A preoccupation with rules and regulations can easily divert our attention from the serious sins in our lives. We can even follow the example of Christians in John's day and regard them as non-existent; or still worse, try to bring other believers into bondage by trying to impose our own personal rules on them! This can result in serious sins being unrecognized and therefore unconfessed, creating a massive build-up of guilt, spoiling relationships and producing unhappiness. This is an inevitable result if you 'Look at the speck of sawdust in your brother's eye and pay no attention to the plank in your own eye' (Matthew 7:3).

Guilty—and expecting to get off scot-free?

Some Christians go to the opposite extreme. They feel that one can sin with impunity without relationships with God or man being affected in the slightest. Lazy and indulgent, they feel that God is satisfied with the fabric of Christianity (Bible reading, church going and praying), and will either ignore or forgive the rest!

Others think of sin as a kind of joke. 'You know me, I'm not the super keen kind of Christian.' They fear becoming too fanatical. They shouldn't worry, they're a million miles from that.

I know that by now Harry, you'll feel I'm being much too severe. And, yes, I do know that you feel both guilty and deeply sorry. But if I'd told you in advance what would happen in the last few months you'd have dismissed it as impossible. So I do want you to understand the roots of sin, and then we'll move to the glorious freedom of forgiveness. It's coming—don't worry. Just let me get this off my chest because there are those who get so caught up in God's grace and mercy that they ignore his absolute standards of holiness and righteousness.

Bob Mumford recently told this story:

> Two prostitutes, one black, the other Spanish, came forward at one of my street rallies. They smiled and said, 'Pray for the Lord's blessing on us. Pray God will help us to help others—to love people.'
>
> Since they were known prostitutes, I said in answer, 'Don't you mean you want me to pray that God will open your eyes to the reality of Christ—so you can be saved and set free from prostitution?'
>
> 'No,' they answered emphatically. 'We are saved. Sure, we are prostitutes, but the Bible says all things are lawful. We enjoy what we do, and God wants us to be happy. We are loved, and we love God, too. To the pure, all things are pure. Our minds are pure, so is our prostitution.'
>
> I could not convince them they were sinners, breakers of the commandments of Christ. Someone had sold them on a message of grace without repentance or separation.
>
> *Plumbline*, Vol. 6, No. 6

Then there are those who believe that if you spend too much time worrying over sin you'll lose your freedom and power. Finally, there are Christians, like some in first century Rome, who believed that the more they sinned the greater would be the opportunity for God to exercise forgiveness! Paul summarizes this particular viewpoint, 'What shall we say, then? Shall we go on sinning, so that grace may increase?' (Romans 6:1). J. B. Phillips paraphrases Paul's horrified reply: 'What a ghastly thought!'

All those who would dismiss sin lightly, or who view it with a kind of benevolent fatalism which says, 'I can't change anyway,' are totally wrong. We are made in God's image, to know, love, obey and walk with him. Failing to do so will mean that we will live in disobedience to God and will harm both ourselves and others.

First of all, because sin results in guilt and guilt inevitably makes you feel dirty.

Now this does not merely concern sexual sins but equally applies to lying, cheating, losing your temper, dishonesty in business, laziness, and even cheating the taxman!

Secondly, we hurt those whom we love, because sin spreads like the most contagious infection. Automatically we harm our fellow-Christians because we get blamed for each other's mistakes. What's more, the guilt-feelings which sin causes are often only relieved by our imposing a sense of failure in those close to us, criticizing them when the fault actually lies in us. Sometimes we embroil other people in our wrongdoings. In the same way when Eve involved Adam in her disobedience, he was quick to pin the blame on her. But as each partner in sin tries to blame the other, they fail to see a watching world taking careful note.

Thirdly, and most important of all, sin clouds our relationship with God. He cannot tolerate sin, so as John points out, 'If we claim to have fellowship with him yet walk in the darkness, we lie and do not live by the truth. But if we walk in the light, as he is in the light, we have fellowship with one another, and the blood of Jesus, his

Son, purifies us from all sin' (1 John 1:6–7).

To make matters worse, God's character, his holiness and purity are the living guarantee that sin must receive its just reward. Those who reject God's unique offer of forgiveness, a gift which demanded the death of his own Son, are solemnly warned that, 'The wages of sin is death.' But eternal separation from God is counter-balanced by the guarantee to all who give their lives as a home for God's Spirit to live and rule within that 'the gift of God is eternal life in Christ Jesus our Lord' (Romans 6:23).

Every time I realize I'm forgiven

While most of us are very clear as to our status as sinners and we recognize the justice of God's condemnation of sin, we find it hard to believe that his heart's longing is that we might know the freedom of being personally forgiven.

When I was a child I always feared heaven. I imagined God with a big black book revealing to my father and friends all of my past indiscretions. The idea that the blood of Jesus actually removes our sins never crossed my mind.

Examine the evidence for a moment. Let's listen to witnesses.

Jesus offered wine to his disciples as a symbol of the fact that 'This is my blood of the covenant, which is poured out for many for the forgiveness of sins' (Matthew 26:28).

Peter issued the challenge for people to turn their lives around and be baptized, 'for the forgiveness of your sins' (Acts 2:38, RSV). Again he emphasized the same point, 'Repent, then, and turn to God so that your sins may be wiped out' (Acts 3:19).

The Psalmist rejoiced in God who 'forgives all my sins

and heals all my diseases' (Psalms 103:3).

Jeremiah said it, and the writer of the letter to the Hebrews repeated it, 'I will forgive . . . and will remember their sins no more' (Jeremiah 31:34).

Jesus triumphantly proclaimed, 'It is finished' as he took your sin and mine upon himself and died so that his blood might give us total and complete forgiveness.

Paul affirms that—'He forgave us all our sins' (Colossians 2:13) and encourages us to 'Forgive as the Lord forgave you' (Colossians 3:13).

John sums it all up: 'If we confess our sins, he is faithful and just and will forgive us our sins and purify us from all unrighteousness' (1 John 1:9).

Satan will try time and time again to live up to his New Testament name of Accuser [see page 34]. So Satan wants us to believe that we can't really be forgiven, we can't really escape ever from what we have been and done. God says that not only are we forgiven, but our sin is forgotten. The future lies ahead and we are already set free from the guilt which is behind us.

Let's put into dialogue form a simple response between God and ourselves:

'Lord, I'm sorry I've done it again.'

'What have you done, my son?'

'Lord, you know what I've done, and I've done it again.'

'What have you done, my son?'

'Lord, you do know, I've done it so often. I keep returning to say sorry, but I've done it again.'

'What have you done, my son? I don't remember.'

If we confess, God has promised his forgiveness. When his Son's blood covers our sins they are completely blotted out in God's sight.

In other words. We're free.

Free of our past.

Free from the tyranny of habit.

Free from guilt and self-blame.

Free to be all that God wants us to be.

Free to be, as A. W. Tozer once said, as holy as a man wants to be.

Not perfect, not totally free from all sin, but certainly free from the bondage and tyranny of sin, so we can get back to living as God always intended we should.

That is why John so quickly encourages new Christians. 'My dear children, I write this to you so that you will not sin. But if anybody does sin, we have one who speaks to the Father in our defence—Jesus Christ, the Righteous One' (1 John 2:1).

Forgiven. Yes, but privilege involves responsibility. We may not shirk our responsibility as we begin to live our whole life as God intends.

'It is required that those who have been given a trust must prove faithful.' The death of Jesus demands that we prove to be different in our attitude to sin—to the root problem, that is, we must not just toy with changes to peripheral actions. When Satan sees us living like that, then the Tempter will arrive. That is not the moment for despair but for triumph, because Satan sees that we're actually worth bothering about! You've been forgiven much, now is the opportunity to begin to live as a forgiven person!

8

Born Losers

It's so hard to face up to failure. Especially when you realize the implications of all that you've done—and that it has all been your fault as well!

Even though I know that I'm forgiven I find that I just can't help feeling scared that it could all happen again.

I never could stand spiritual schizophrenics. You know, the hypocrites who claim to be one thing and yet live as if they were something else entirely. Such people were a breed which I found pretty hard to stomach. So I'm pretty sickened about how close I've come to being like that myself.

The cold fact of the matter is that I've determined that I really do want to serve God with all of my life. I've seen too many miserable Christians who look as if they are in two minds over the issue of God's rule. One part of their lives is surrendered to Jesus Christ while the rest remains firmly under their own control. In other words they go about like 'a walking civil war'!

Trouble is that I can recognize all the agonies which adopting that kind of lifestyle must inevitably cause. It must be self-torture, trying to fool yourself. Pretending to be something that you're not. Living a Jekyll and

*Hyde existence and torn both ways. Two mutually ex-
clusive existences with guilt and remorse the only bedfellows allowed. I want nothing to do with it. I've made
my choices and have no inclination to change my mind.*

*What worries me is how close I've come to doing
everything that I wanted to avoid while barely realizing
I'd even started going down the slippery slope. I'm not
trying to pass the buck or avoid the blame. I'd been
given the classic do's and don'ts but before I'd realized
what was going on I'd started on the wrong road.*

*Now I know we haven't seen each other for months
but I wondered if you could attempt some explanations.
I know that most of it will be theory but I suspect that
you'll shed a lot of light on those areas where I can
honestly say, 'no-one ever told me'.*

Please help—I feel guilty.

*I kind of feel that I need some spiritual backbone—a
new understanding of what's happening to me. Even
though I really believe that I've turned my back on all
that was going on the last few months I can hardly
believe that history won't repeat itself. I still feel the
same emotional pulls, those withdrawal symptoms when I
look at the old lifestyle, the areas of weakness where
things don't really seem to be improving.*

*Your last treatise helped me such a lot. I feel like a
load has been lifted from my shoulders. What's more,
you've made me realize a whole number of things which
I'd either forgotten or ignored. I now know the exhilar-
ating sense of being forgiven—but I don't want to just
take advantage and go backwards again!*

*The problem is, the day after your letter, I had to face
up to all those attitudes which I've been secretly tolerat-
ing for too long. Is temptation permanent? Must I always fail when I meet up with it? Do things ever get
easier or must it always be like this?*

I feel such a failure and I really don't want to just

stagger from one spiritual crisis to the next.

When I was at theological college, the end of the course climaxed in the local version of the death of a thousand cults. Each student had to preach a sermon to the assembled student body as a foretaste of all an unsuspecting world would receive in a few weeks' time!

I chose to share about Peter's denial of Jesus. I talked of the inevitable failure which must meet all Christians in their attempts to serve God. I expressed the, to me, inescapable conclusion that failure was God's normal plan for his people. By taking that line I joined a long succession of Christian pragmatists—who got it all wrong!

Just as a Parliamentary law has later to be verified by the appropriate authority, so the victory won by Jesus has to become a living reality in the lives of Christians. In Matthew 28, Jesus stated that all power was his, and he instructed his church to go into the world carrying that authority. Jesus came to destroy the Devil's work (1 John 3:8), and as a result of his disarming him (Colossians 2:15), Christians can now enjoy the benefits of what he did. We don't have to fight *for* a position of victory over Satan but *from* it. The sequence of teaching in Ephesians illustrates this. The blessings and security in Christ come at the beginning, and at the end there is the battle.

Some would polarize this issue by demanding that we either see ourselves as perfect (i.e. victors), or imperfect (i.e. failures). That is a far from correct conclusion. From time to time my children fail to behave as part of the family. Now that does not make them orphans, nor are their actions unforgiveable. But neither are they to be excused. Forgiveness is basic to family life. Perfection doesn't come naturally to children. Saying sorry and being brought back into the heart of the family is a regular occurrence. This does not indicate that children are failures. It's just a natural part of their development, some aspects of which they will learn to grow out of!

What is more, when it comes to change, we have everything going for us. We need to remind ourselves that we are more than just imitators of Christ. It's true that he is a model to follow, but that's only one aspect of it. He also personally indwells as through the Spirit, assuring us of his presence and enabling in all situations. We are also equipped with the mighty two-edged sword of the Spirit, the Bible, for personal growth and for battle. Above all, we have direct access to God through the medium of prayer which is always available to us. In fact, we never walk alone.

The temptation is always there to disbelieve that fact; to allow confusion, loneliness and unbelief to undermine the simple childlike trust which Jesus has commended us to have. Now that is exactly how you're feeling at the moment. You have failed and the question which keeps coming back is how you'll avoid failure next time. Meanwhile at every level of your life, and everyone else's for that matter, you experience temptation, and that just enhances your sense of insecurity.

Tempted to go for success.

Tempted to wallow in self-pity.

Tempted to hurt and damage others.

Tempted to give up.

Tempted to run away.

Tempted to put it off.

Tempted to accept the wrong invitation.

Tempted to trust the wrong people.

Tempted to go your own way.

It's so easy to believe that temptation is in fact sin, but the tempting offer is there to be accepted, or avoided. In other words, we're being put to the test. Temptation of itself is neutral: it is our response which brings either sin or blessing. Temptation does not mean that we're in awful sin; it's our response to it that decides that. After all, as Paul reminded the Corinthian church, 'No temptation has seized you except what is common to man.' What is more, he goes on to encourage them to recognize that 'God is faithful; he will not let you be tempted beyond what you can bear. But when you are tempted, he will also provide a way out so that you can stand up under it' (1 Corinthians 10:13).

When you ask if there is an inevitability about the temptation, then the answer has to be 'yes'. God allows that temptation but not so that we might be dragged under by it. Instead he supplies the resources that we might overcome it and be both matured and encouraged by the experience—bitter though it may be at the time!

However, I'm slightly evading the issue because your questions probe to the heart of why it is so easy to fall for the temptation!

Breaking the rules

New sports are constantly developing. The latest addition to the Olympic programme is windsurfing. It is a difficult sport to learn and one where it is very easy to break the rules. One obvious way is by artificially 'pumping' the sail in order to go faster; it seems okay—until you're spotted doing it! Every windsurfer gets tempted to break the rules but penalties are only handed out if he gives in to the temptation.

Temptation is quite normal and is to be expected if we are growing with God. It must also be quite usual for us to resist and avoid the sin to which we are being drawn. What makes our position hazardous is if we are already slightly bending the rules. 'Borrowing' from our place of work easily becomes theft. Cheating on the tax form quickly develops into tax evasion. Chatting up an attractive girl can become adultery for a married man, before he's even recognized the danger. And it all begins by bending the rules.

Starting right

Sin rarely 'just happens'. Satan doesn't often present us with a major challenge which we can dramatically refuse. Instead he gradually erodes our confidence, creating guilt at a thousand smaller failures.

Often at the root of our feelings of guilt lies the suspicion that by breaking the rules we are sowing the seed of our own destruction.

King David was very like that. Self-indulgence gripped him and the evil results became sadly inevitable. We often think that King David suddenly succumbed to Satan's whispers as he gazed at the lovely Bathsheba taking her bath in the twilight. 'You are the king, why shouldn't you do as you like just this once?' But that once wasn't enough. David then wanted to possess her permanently, and he ensured that her husband Uriah was killed in battle. Once sinful activities commenced, things swiftly escalated from bad to worse. Lust moved to adultery, adultery to murder. Yet it all had its beginning in the rules which David broke:

(1) 'In the spring, at the time when kings go off to war, David sent Joab out with the king's men and the whole Israelite army. They destroyed the Ammonites and besieged Rabbah. But David remained in Jerusalem' (2 Samuel 11:1). In other words David was in the wrong place at the wrong time. He was failing to fulfil his duties and responsibilities as King. He should have been leading the army, but left that job to Joab, his commander-in-chief.

(2) 'One evening David got up from his bed and walked around on the roof of the palace. From the roof he saw a woman bathing' (2 Samuel 11:2). In his own

laziness and indolence David had time on his hands and allowed his eyes to wander.

(3) 'The King, moreover, must not acquire great numbers of horses for himself. . . . He must not take many wives, or his heart will be led astray. He must not accumulate large amounts of silver and gold' (Deuteronomy 17:16–17). Those had been the instructions from God. In fact David had deserted the rustic simplicity of Saul's court for a much wealthier and ostentatious display which served to prepare the way for Solomon. He acquired horses and, 'In Jerusalem David took more wives' (1 Chronicles 14:3). He deserted instructions and prepared the ground for sin to follow.

(4) 'Satan rose up against Israel and incited David to take a census of Israel. . . . This command was also evil in the sight of God' (1 Chronicles 21:1, 7). One thing leads to another and the sin with Bathsheba only served to open the door for Satan.

(5) 'You shall not covet your neighbour's wife' (Exodus 20:17). But David broke all the rules, even the most straightforward ones, and ruined his life. It is also quite clear that Satan was behind this initiative. He always will attack the people of God, wherever we break the rules and offer him the opportunity.

When I was a child, a shoe company used their trade name to good advertising advantage in Underground stations. Their slogan read 'Startrite (the brand name), and you'll walk happily ever after.' Satan could well parody the phrase, 'Start wrong and you'll have hell to pay'!

The hardest word in the world

And it only has two letters. Yet it has proved to be amazingly difficult to use at the very time when it is most valuable and appropriate.

Saying 'no' is hardly fashionable today. It breaks all the rules of contemporary society where anything goes. But how much trouble we could save ourselves if only we would resist Satan's promptings with that one simple word. As Alexandra Ross wrote:

> There is something in the corrupt heart of man, 'his own desire', which responds to the bait which has been so cunningly placed in the trap of temptation by the arch enemy of our souls. He is beguiled and allured by his own desire, attracted by the bait!
> *Commentary on the Epistles of James and John* (Eerdmans)

James illustrates the mechanics of temptation by referring to the world of hunting and fishing (James 1:14). A fish is safe and secure so long as it stays in its hole under the river bank. A skilful fisherman has to find a way of luring it from its place of safety so that he may hook it and subject it to his will. He does this by using bait of some kind, like an artificial fly or a wriggling maggot. The fish, attracted by the bait, abandons common sense; it leaves the safety of its hole. Only when it's firmly hooked does it realize that it has been outwitted by the fisherman and that it will soon be sizzling in the frying pan.

This is how Satan uses temptation. The secure place for the Christian is resting in the presence and will of God, focusing only on what is pleasing to him, and being nourished, guided and cared for by the Giver of good and perfect gifts (James 1:17). Satan's plan is to use a bait which will lure the Christian away from the safe hiding place, and then hook him so that he will do something which is displeasing to God.

Just as a fisherman has many kinds of bait and knows just which to use on each occasion, so Satan chooses his bait carefully. After all, he's got quite a variety to choose from. But all we have to say is one word, 'No.'

An American pastor was a long way from home, alone in a Canadian hotel. He entered a lift to go up to his room. Two attractive girls were already in the lift. They eyed him up and down.

'Which floor?' one of them asked.

'Six,' he replied. 'And for you?'

'Oh, six will do fine,' they laughed in reply. 'It'll be fun.'

The struggle of saying no faced him squarely in the face. He was miles from home. After all, only God would ever know. He said it, and turned his back on the temptation.

There are so many things that require our saying no. We may be challenged to meet our needs in the wrong way, to think wrong thoughts or to misuse things or principles entrusted to us. But whether the temptation is to follow the 'lust of the eyes', or to give in to the 'lusts of the flesh', or demonstrate arrogance in the 'pride of life'; God has one answer for us—a two letter word. Learning how to say it, and where to use it, will require a courage that few of us believe we have until we pause to remember that we are not alone and that God himself will provide the resources with which we can say no.

I'm still standing!

Well, just. Because as usual it was a close run thing.

It was the fifth test. No, not a cricket series, but an average hour in a normal morning. First was the temptation to turn over and go back to sleep again. Then the desire to strangle the children, who were re-enacting their own live version of Star Wars in the small bedroom. Third, was the tendency to scream when the Corn Flakes packet was empty and the milk boiled over. The fourth test involved the search for the missing car keys. The last straw was a potent desire to kick the car when it wouldn't start. Enough was enough!

Today we tend to regard 'temptation' as always representing a push towards bad actions rather than good ones. But the original meaning was simply 'to test'. So temptation is neither good nor evil but essentially neutral. Results can be good or bad depending on who is doing the testing, and the response we make to the demands being made upon us.

A girl suffered from anorexia nervosa. In the psychiatric ward of the local hospital temptation was a regular part of the treatment. Privilege and inducements were offered for each weight addition. In other words temptation was all there for her own benefit.

The point is important because both God and Satan use testing to achieve their purposes in the lives of God's people. While God's motives are always good and are designed for the strengthening of believers, Satan invariably has bad intentions because his chief aim is to ruin Christian lives.

If we expand James 1:14 then much is illuminated for us. 'But each one is tempted when, by his own evil desire' (heavily distorted and exaggerated by Satan) 'he is dragged away' (from the security of being in God's will) 'and enticed' (to swallow the bait held out by Satan and made extraordinarily attractive to our enlarged desires). 'Then, after desire has conceived' (in us—not everybody else) 'it gives birth to sin;' (for which we are responsible) 'and sin, when it is full-grown,' (it tends to expand—one leads to another) 'gives birth to death' (the tragic result!).

We always like to excuse ourselves and blame others —unfortunately for us the Bible does not leave us with that kind of loophole.

My first ever job was as an invoice clerk during the summer vacation for a TV repair workshop. Now the rules said, 'Never carry more than one television set on the trolley.' But everyone took two, three or four and so did I. But one devastating afternoon I lost my grip on the second set and it went crashing from the trolley to the concrete floor!

'It wasn't my fault, it was an accident.'

The excuse was so glib and natural. So was the reply. 'Then why were you breaking the rules? If you hadn't it would never have happened.'

In one sense it wasn't my fault. I never intended to break the TV; but it was my fault for breaking the rules!

Man and the mousetrap

In a recent Test match against England the opposition captain used a combined attack of a fast bowler and a spinner. The former used speed, accuracy and some nasty bouncers to remove the batsman. The spinner, on the other hand, bowled very slowly, enticing the batsman to hit out, hoping he would offer a catch in the slips. When Satan uses temptation he is acting like the spinner. It is subtlety and deception which do the damage.

Satan's traps are always individually designed to fit our personal weaknesses. He knows our danger-points and cleverly frames his attacks in exactly those directions. His traps are always carefully concealed. After all, who ever heard of a mousetrap boldly labelled, *eat here, pay later*!

All Satan has to do is to seduce us away from our love for God into breaking the rules. In his letter to Timothy Paul describes people who have fallen into Satan's trap and have been 'Taken captive to do his will' (2 Timothy 2:26). Anyone who does Satan's will cannot be doing what God wants. God and Satan want totally committed followers whose only desire is to obey their master. Temptation is designed to draw us as far away as possible from total allegiance to God.

Satan had that in mind for you. But his plan has back-fired. After all Jesus has won the victory for us. Failure is Satan's province not ours. Having learned the lesson it's important to build a new platform for the future. Don't write, I'm out of hours and paper but I want to continue on this theme—so for the time being don't start raising other matters and complicating the issue. Next time we'll look at the foundations for moving forward.

9

Escape into Victory

I'm sorry—it's rare I disagree with you, but frankly I'm still confused. A friend of mine was taking a meeting recently, and he posed a clever question.

'Please raise your hand if you've lived today free from conscious sin.'

One or two brave hands were raised.

'Please raise your hand if you've lived the last hour free from conscious sin.'

More hands went up.

'Please raise your hand if you've lived the last minute free from conscious sin.'

A forest of hands shot up.

'If you can do it for a minute, why not a day?'

Silence. My friend had made his point. God's way for his people must be one of increasing victory rather than steady defeat.

The question is, what's your reaction when I say that I still feel defeated? I know that's only me condemning myself, I know it's not true, but I still feel that way.

We readily agree with the apostle Paul that, 'When I want to do good, evil is right there with me. For in my inner being I delight in God's law; but I see another law at work in the members of my body, waging war against the law of my mind and making me a prisoner of the law of sin' (Romans 7:21–23). Paul cries out, 'Who will rescue me from this body of death?' But then triumphantly answers his own question. 'Thanks be to God—through Jesus Christ our Lord!' (Romans 7:24–25).

Harry, your reaction may be to say, 'That's fine in theory, but it doesn't work in practice!' As far as we're concerned (and that went for Paul too) we should be enjoying victory not defeat. If we were committing wilful sin, deliberately disregarding God's commands, not praying, reading our Bibles, or working hard for God, then we'd expect to fail. As in Paul's case, when you're doing your level best for God it seems so unfair that things should go wrong. It would be understandable if our failures came as a result of not coping with a major personal crisis, a sudden Satanic attack, or an unexpected temptation.

The tensions which so many of us feel because of the desires of our mind and the resultant wrong attitudes and actions, are experienced by many Christians. These tensions are caused by the fierce battle which continues inside us. 'I see another law at work in the members of my body, waging war against the law of my mind' (Romans 7:23). Satan wants to use our sinful natures to drag us down. God wants to lift us up and set us free to live holy lives for him.

If the real ambition of your heart is to love and serve the living God, then there are four basic lessons which must be learned and appreciated. These will act as a firm foundation, helping you to break with the past and enter into the future which God has for you.

Step 1—Don't pass the buck

How often I hear the words—it's not my fault!

When Mary Dekker tripped over Zola Budd's feet in the final of the 3,000 metres at the Los Angeles Olympics in 1984, there was immediate furore. Somehow it was always someone else's fault.

There is nothing unusual in that. When Adam and Eve first sinned in the Garden of Eden their thoughts revolved around how to pass the buck so that someone else received the blame.

Guilt always demands punishment but we always try to break the rules by evading our own responsibilities.

(a) God, it's your fault

'The woman you put here with me' (Genesis 3:12). If you hadn't given me the woman it would all never have happened. Often it is all too easy to blame God for our temptations, but James points out, 'God cannot be tempted by evil, nor does he tempt anyone' (James 1:13). One suspects that among those to whom he was writing there were some who were blaming God because they had fallen into sin. To such people James wrote, 'Don't be deceived. . . . Every good and perfect gift is from above, coming down from the Father of the heavenly lights, who does not change like shifting shadows' (1:16–17). God is not two-faced, providing good things one minute, then tempting us to do evil the next. James compares that kind of inconsistent behaviour with shifting shadows. God is one hundred per cent reliable, he never cheats or deceives his children.

(b) The Devil made me do it

'The serpent deceived me, and I ate' (Genesis 3:13). For many of us that has become little more than a convenient excuse for our own self-indulgence. In fact, I'm sure Satan would be delighted if he were guilty of half of which he is accused!

Yet he certainly is guilty of doing all that he can to

direct us towards sin. In Eden he succeeded in feeding Eve's imagination with many reasons why she should eat what God had forbidden, and the more she chewed it over in her mind, the more she wanted to take the bait. As Moffat wrote, sin is 'the imagination toying with a forbidden idea, and then issuing in a decision of the will'.

When we are deceived into following those wrongly nourished desires and we swallow the bait set by Satan, it results in an act of sin. When our wills obey wrong desires, then those wills are entering into an unhealthy alliance with our desires, and spawned from that unfortunate marriage comes the inevitable offspring—sin.

In today's society, someone has to be held responsible for everything that goes wrong. Those who suffer innocently are entitled to react bitterly and to receive compensation. The offender has to be punished. Very little emphasis is placed on personal responsibility. It has largely been displaced by the desire to claim one's rights from others. The result is that many people have become lazy, spineless and irresponsible because there's always someone else to bear the burden, whether it be an individual or the state.

This may seem to be something of a cynical overreaction. Yet we live at a time when an American President, caught in the act, fails to admit guilt and say, 'I was wrong, I'm sorry.' In fact, those words look like dying out through lack of usage!

Christians are in danger of adopting the same attitudes. We wrote earlier about the seventies being the great ME era. This has led to some of us thinking that we only need to serve God faithfully when things are going our way. Our failures? Well, we feel perfectly justified in shifting the blame or finding a reasonable excuse.

'God led me into a temptation I couldn't resist.'

'Satan's schemes were so subtle that I couldn't help falling.'

'My old nature got the better of me.'

'My church doesn't provide the support and teaching I need.'

'How can I be victorious when everything is going wrong around me like illness, unemployment and family problems?'

'God hasn't equipped me as well as other people.'

'I'm a hurt person because of my upbringing. I haven't the strength to be victorious. I have too many personal problems.'

'God has put me in a career which leaves me too little time to pray, read the Bible or serve. I shall have to leave that to others.'

Does it sound a little familiar?

I could add to this list, but I won't. Harry, if you feel as if your life is spiritually barren at the moment you too may have tried to explain it away. Let me ask you a rather direct question: 'Is it right to accept defeat simply because there's always a reasonable explanation for why you fall? It will greatly help us if we see things from God's perspective instead of just through our own somewhat biased eyes!

We need to realize that God holds us responsible. Way back in the garden God put the blame squarely on Adam and Eve. Clearly there were strong pressures to succumb to Satan's smooth talking, but with God's help they need never have fallen flat on their faces!

I only wish that more Christians would accept responsibility for their own actions. However, when you do, then you run into the parallel problem: it becomes so easy to sink into depression over your own shortcomings. It is crucial that we give God our failures so that he can bring us freedom and forgiveness from all our weakness and guilt.

Step 2: Receive God's caring response

The Gospels give us a vivid description of this in the story of *Rocky*—the original version.

Long before Sylvester Stallone's movies, 'Rocky' was Jesus' nickname for his front running disciple, Simon Peter. Here was a stubborn, pig-headed fisherman who always led with his chin. On one memorable evening he boldly asserted that even when everyone else showed their true colours he would never fail to stand by Jesus, yet within hours he had failed on no less than three successive occasions.

What did Jesus do with his prize failure? Three denials produced three responses from Jesus.

(1) 'The Lord turned and looked straight at Peter. Then Peter remembered' (Luke 22:61). There's never any escape from our actions. Jesus didn't pretend that it wasn't important. With just a look he made Peter face up to his failure and sin. This was not an act of spite on the part of Jesus. He required tears of repentance from Peter, not that he might be mortified by personal guilt but so that he could be forgiven!

(2) 'He is not here. See the place where they laid him. But go, tell his disciples and Peter' (Mark 16:6–7). Good news of resurrection, but a special emphasis is placed on Peter being told. Why is he singled out? Because having ministered conviction to Peter, Jesus now wants to see him be well and truly encouraged!

(3) 'Simon son of John, do you truly love me. . . . Feed my lambs' (John 21:15). Now we come to the third response from Jesus to the three failures of Peter. This time Jesus challenged Peter on the depth of commitment in his relationship to Jesus. This is immediately followed by a challenge to stop looking in and to begin to look outward to the needs of others.

Some of us become paranoid about our own failures.

We punish ourselves either physically or emotionally.
But we do not have the right to do so. If we have surrendered our lives to Jesus, then punishment or commen-
dation belong to him alone. Hurting ourselves is a response to Satan's temptations; it cannot honour God. His
judgements are righteous, while our punishment of ourselves is always arbitrary.

Jesus' method of dealing with Peter was quite straightforward—conviction, encouragement, then the challenge to commitment and witness, that he might go on
living and not continue in failure. Jesus' words to the
woman caught in the act of adultery demonstrate the
same approach. Conviction and encouragement are followed by the challenge: 'Go now and leave your life of
sin' (John 8:11).

What is more, Peter must have been continually amazed that he didn't have to struggle on alone. After all,
knowing all that was going to happen, Jesus had told him
in no uncertain fashion, 'Simon, Simon, Satan has asked
to sift you as wheat. But I have prayed for you, Simon,
that you may not fail. And when you have turned back,
strengthen your brothers' (Luke 22:31–32). Isn't it amazing that even in your failure Jesus is praying for you,
preparing your future, and making sure that there is *always a way back*. You can never fall so far that the Lord
isn't longing to welcome you home.

Step 3: Recognize the divorce

The trouble is that whenever we live under an external
code or rule something inside us—our sinful nature—
wants to use that rule to make us appear failures.

Our sinful nature begins to dominate whenever we try
to live our Christian lives by slavishly obeying a set of
rules and regulations. This even applies to Biblical demands. We cannot reach God's standards in our own

strength. To live under the law is to allow sin to gain control again. But, as Paul reminds us, 'Sin shall not be your master, because you are not under law, but under grace' (Romans 6:14).

Our old marriage to the law has to be dissolved in order that we might be free to relate fully to God, and enjoy all the freedom that Jesus has died to give us. From God's side, this divorce has already taken place; now it's our turn. 'By dying to what once bound us, we have been released from the law so that we serve in the new way of the Spirit' (Romans 7:6). So many Christians are still living as though that old marriage still existed— by treating the Christian life as if it consisted largely of keeping a set of rules and regulations. It's like getting a divorce from that nagging wife (the law), marrying someone else (Christ: 'that you might belong to another, to him who was raised from the dead' [7:4], then reuniting with the ex-wife. You end up having two wives at the same time, trying to please both, and discovering that it can't be done.

Spiritual bigamy is just not allowed!

Many non-Christians see life as attempting to do enough good acts to outweigh our bad. Sadly, we can see the Christian life in the same way. But it is quite clear that our human natures can't serve God. Only the Holy Spirit can perform in our lives those things which will delight Jesus. We cannot earn our way to heaven. The number of meetings we attend, prayers we offer or good deeds we perform will never impress the living God. It is as our sinful lives are covered by the blood of his Son and empowered and renewed by his Spirit that our divorce from fleshly ability is made complete. Then we live by and through his power alone.

Step 4: Surrender to a new king

Suddenly Paul's cry of despair, 'What a wretched man I am! Who will rescue me?' is transformed into a shout of victory. 'Thanks be to God—through Jesus Christ our Lord' (Romans 7:24–25).

It all clicks into place. In the middle of his turmoil and confusion he recognizes that the answer lies not in human effort but in Jesus Christ! The answer stares us in the face—right there in our Bibles. Yet sadly many Christians today have reached that same point of desperation but missed the solution.

We must recognize that we can never serve God through our own efforts.

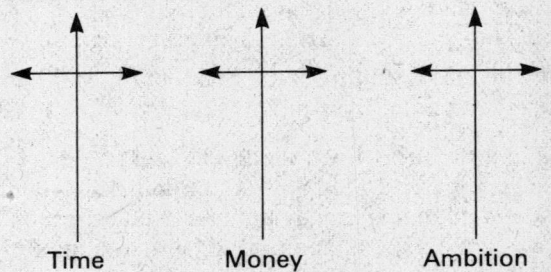

Time   Money   Ambition

When our will for our lives (horizontal line) crosses God's will for our lives (vertical line) we surrender our way to his, God wins and can point our lives in the direction which he has for them. In the same way, our attempts to live and act for God in our own strength must be subordinated to him. Then as our intrusive nature steps back the Holy Spirit can move and act through us.

The difference is dramatic. Our words are replaced by his. Our actions by his. Our ambitions by his. Our strategy by his. Each day we learn to surrender more and more to him, each day we learn to live more by his power and less by our own.

Forgiven failures

Peter did not live a perfect life, failure-free, from the time of Jesus' ascension onwards. He struggled with prejudice, politics and Paul. In fact Peter and Paul had a stand-up confrontation with each other. Yet he was mightily used by God who brought thousands to himself through 'Rocky'. Peter has learned certain lessons but that did not make him perfect. However, he was prepared to go on being forgiven, and to go on learning. The next time that he was tempted to deny Jesus, the results were very different. 'They were astonished, and they took note that these men had been with Jesus' (Acts 4:13). Even when they were threatened by the authorities, Peter and his colleague, John, refused to compromise. 'Judge for yourselves whether it is right in God's sight to obey you rather than God. For we cannot help speaking about what we have seen and heard' (Acts 4:19-20).

What a difference! Even though he still failed in other areas he had learned a lesson from his failure to stand up for Jesus—and that is exactly how we need to respond to *our* failures. We miss the point if we sink into indifference or self-condemnation. God wants us to recognize his forgiveness and desires that we learn a lesson—and don't do it again!

Noah, Abraham, Elijah, Jonah, Thomas—on goes God's hall of fame—and all of them forgiven failures! Time and again God uses our mistakes to teach and train us—so that we become far more effective and useful in his service.

It is easy to argue that my failures can never end, that the problems I face are too great. But God's commands to us are very clear. We are not at liberty to decide that victory is not possible because circumstances are against us. In New Testament days Paul told the Philippians to:

'continue to work out your salvation' (2:12) even though he was not there to guide them, in fact, especially because he was not there. Even though the days were described by Paul as evil the Ephesians were told to 'understand what the Lord's will is' (5:17). 'But I can't,' we protest. To that Paul replies that before we conclude failure is inevitable we must remember it is 'God who works in you to will and to act according to his good purpose' (Philippians 2:13). With him nothing is impossible!

Those who are the most determined will usually see the greatest changes in their lives, which will often happen at greater speeds. I can recall two men in their thirties who sought my help after a rally in London. I offered suggestions to both and prayed with each man separately. One followed them up and changed radically within six months. The other was too lazy and indifferent to do anything, and when we met accidentally two years later he was still the same.

Some barriers, like emotional hurts, need the sensitive and skilled help of a competent counsellor. Others require sheer naked guts and single-minded effort. When Jesus said, 'Follow me', the cost was too high for some. The rich young ruler went away sad and unchanged. A teacher of the law thought he wanted to follow Jesus but it required a willingness to face the insecurity of being homeless. Other barriers to wholehearted commitment were the purchase of a field, marriage, and the unwillingness to leave home before the death of a father. Each man had the opportunity of being a follower but decided against it.

At the heart of the Christian message lies the inescapable fact that on the cross Jesus destroyed the bondage of sin and restored freedom of choice to those who committed their lives to him. Just as Joshua faced up to the question of whom he would serve, and then had to live with the need to make actions consistent with that choice

so we must face the same challenge: 'Choose for yourselves this day whom you will serve' (Joshua 24:15).

The idea that failure involves a conscious choice 'to
do' or 'not to do' is terribly unpopular today. Many regard it as tyrannical and hard-hearted to say that we
choose to sin. Yet others have found joy and freedom in
recognizing that we no longer need to go on sinning. We
just don't have to!

You have the choice

Nowadays great emphasis is laid on our having freedom
to choose. Jesus died to destroy the power of sin and
death, and we can choose to use or misuse the freedom
he gave us. Choice applies in each area of our lives. But
often liberty has run riot and degenerated into wild
licence. Many have determined that in today's society
we are,

> Free to choose, to earn your loaf,
> To sleep with him, or her, or both.
> Calver/Oliver, 'Getting it together' (CPO, 1971)

However, we are not only free to choose to do, but
also to abstain. I was recently involved in a committee
with a number of tremendous Christians working with
homosexuals, transvestites, trans-sexuals and lesbians.
The key word in their ministry was *choice*.

Christians differ greatly from each other! Just look at
the contrasts between you and me! That variety is also
expressed in the way that we grow in our spiritual lives.
Some make gradual progress without ever facing up to
huge crises or having to make major decisions. They
seem to have found the secret of success without really
being aware of taking any definite steps to achieve it.
Most of us, however, move forward in a series of jumps
as we are confronted with new and important issues. For

us, the fact that Christ's work is complete and we have been given the Spirit doesn't automatically assure us of victory. Many of us will remain trapped by the tyranny of self-effort until we are willing to establish a more positive relationship with God's Spirit.

The decision which faces us concerns a choice between two conflicting control centres competing for our lives. Each desires to win. Satan longs for us to be content to live under law by our own self-effort. God wants us to trust his Spirit. The two can never co-exist peacefully within a life. 'For the sinful nature desires what is contrary to the Spirit, and the Spirit what is contrary to the sinful nature' (Galatians 5:17).

We can choose to live by human nature and find that we 'cannot please God' (Romans 8:8) or to enjoy 'life and peace' (Romans 8:6) as God's Spirit continually sets us free. It is totally illogical to neglect God's provision because if we do it will result in failure day after day, year after year. That's why Paul was so exasperated with the 'foolish Galatians'. Instead of freedom they let themselves 'be burdened again by a yoke of slavery' (Galatians 5:1). Continually Paul tried to get it into their thick heads that what they were doing would never work. The only solution was to invite the Holy Spirit to take control and to cease their futile efforts at trying to live the Christian life their way.

Let me illustrate this. A few years ago my wife and I wanted to have a door leading from the garage to the kitchen. There had been a door previously but after its removal the hole had been filled in with plaster-board. We removed it quite easily and fitted the door frame using six inch masonry nails. It looked fine until we tried to move the door into the opening. It didn't fit! The door was the right shape but the frame was nowhere near square. There was only one choice—the whole thing would have to be started again. I couldn't pull the nails out and the best I could do was to saw through each of them using a hacksaw blade inserted between the frame and the brickwork. It took three hours of sweat and toil. What I didn't know was that all the banging and sawing had made the brickwork loose. As we removed the frame, bricks began to fall on our heads and the wall started to collapse. That was it—finished—end of project —never again! Utterly defeated, angry and exhausted we decided to employ a local joiner. Because he knew what he was doing he fitted the frame, hung the door and repaired the wall in a matter of hours. Our pride and our bank balance now hurt but the finished product was superb.

There is only one person who can provide the ability to live the Christian life—it is God. When we hand over our lives to the Spirit's control he does things through us in a far superior way to our miserable self-effort. He won't normally force himself on us, but he patiently awaits our invitation for him to take a more active role within us.

In other words, the key to our success lies in the extent to which we are prepared to rest in, and draw from, our relationship with Jesus.

Please help—I feel guilty

They were your words, but so many of us can identify with them. While planning this reply I asked a friend if she knew any illustrations of failure in everyday life. 'Try mine, for a start,' she jokingly replied. But behind her words lay that fear that so many of us have, that in fact we will miss our destiny, for we have failed and can never regain the ground, or the days, which we have lost.

Now there are many dangers in the power of positive thinking. It can develop into little more than well-intentioned humanism. But the opposite is equally not

Christian and can be far more discouraging.

We must never allow past failures to paralyse us into thinking that we can never be useful to God. Many great men and women of the Bible made mistakes but they, like the apostle Paul, were prepared to put the past behind them in order to exercise their will to achieve all that God wanted for their lives. 'But one thing I do: forgetting what is behind and straining towards what is ahead, I press towards the goal' (Philippians 3:13–14).

Consistency in victory and strength to win the bigger and more prolonged battles only come through steady effort. We need to make up our minds to do what we know to be right simply because God says so. If we decide to wait for our emotions to agree before we take action, we may wait for ever. We must expect that there will be failures as well as successes, but we must be prepared to put the past behind us.

Yesterday can never be retrieved, but tomorrow can be relieved of the deficit balance from bygone days if we will only forgive ourselves for past mistakes and begin to look forward to a different kind of future. Long after God has forgiven us we continue to punish ourselves for sins which through the blood of Jesus have been long-forgotten.

In our world negativism and depression are unfortunate facts of life. This does not mean that as Christians we should be the same! We need to approach our Christian lives with optimism rather than pessimism. We must not dwell on the reasons why we feel we can't win but put all our efforts into discovering which route we must take to avoid failure.

It is equally wrong to rely on one particular past victory or vital spiritual experience to keep us going for ever. God has much more to do in us yet and we must be willing to go on learning, changing and maturing.

She knew all this in theory but as a young seventeen-

year-old tears were her normal expression whenever
God was speaking to her. She found it absolutely impossible to believe that she could be forgiven for all that she
had done. Now her situation was very serious and she
found it almost impossible to talk about it. Eventually
everything spilled out. Her pastor and I began to pray
through the things which lay submerged in her past. We
finished. Her head lifted, and sunshine returned to her
face. Past was now past, the future lay ahead.

That kind of freedom is something which many of us
need—and not just on a one-off basis! In fact, if we want
to be really useful to God and to our fellow Christians
then we must keep on learning that failure is not
unforgiveable! Only then will we gain the courage to go
out on a limb with God and engage in that kind of risky
living which lies at the heart of true Christian disciple-
ship.

It all comes down to the motive. The story is told of
the American pastor who receives a regular phone call
from a friend on a Monday morning. (The time when
most preachers re-evaluate Sunday's ministry).

'Hello, this is God. I'm giving you my personal per-
mission to fail.'

The release which that call gives to him is quite incredible. Risks can be taken which would otherwise have
presented him with insurmountable obstacles, tightness
of heart, and a weight on the shoulder, all because failure is permissible where our actions are for God's glory
and the motivation is right!

Free to fail? Yes . . . definitely. But not to make a
habit of it!

After all, Jesus has died to provide us with an ongoing
escape, into victory. Step by step, going further and
getting closer!

10

Believe It or Not

Sometimes I do find it hard to believe all that has hap-
pened over the last few weeks. I'm really grateful for
your help and at last I'm beginning to look forward to
the future.

Things are exciting in the whole range of friendships
and activities at church. We've even taken over a ware-
house which is being converted into a drop-in centre for
the unemployed and a youth outreach centre. There are
about a dozen of us involved in the project and it has
been great to see how the whole thing has come together.

The PCC have been really helpful and the whole
church has been praying and believing that God will
use the centre to bring many people to commit their
lives to him. I've never seen the vicar so excited and I'm
really looking forward to getting stuck into it.

The only big problem that we've had to face is a
financial one. Even after we had all promised the max-
imum financial contributions possible we still are several
thousands of pounds short of what is needed.

The church has met together in order to fast and pray
and the decision has been taken to go ahead 'in faith'.
In other words we are going out on a limb because we
do feel that it is the right thing to do. The only thing

which worries us is this shortfall and I did wonder if you felt that we were being financially irresponsible, spiritually faithful, or a bit of both?

One of the church fellowship is a working evangelist who 'lives by faith'. Time and again I've seen God provide for his needs in remarkable ways. It's thrown up a lot of interest in the church, particularly now that we're all dependent on God's provision in this particular instance.

All in all I've become increasingly fascinated by the whole subject of faith.

I feel that it is often a word that those of us who feel as if we are just very ordinary Christians use very glibly without understanding what really lies behind it. Could you fill in some background and explain what it is that hinders faith? Why is 'simple faith' so denigrated by some church leaders, and how far should faith go?

Faith is a word that is often bandied about and I would certainly value some comment and direction about it all. I've heard the words used as an excuse for not bothering to do what could be done. But I believe that we've approached everyone we can and done all that is possible—now are we right to expect the Lord to cover our needs, or are we just building castles in the air? There is a sense in which our Christian lives are too visible and predictable but I know from all that I've read and seen in other Christian testimonies that there is another dimension.

The Bible is quite specific. Without faith it is actually impossible to please God. Our heavenly Father responds to the simple trust of his earthly children. Just as I love to feel the touch of my son's hand and look into his trusting eyes as he grasps the hand of Daddy, so the living God longs to see our faith at work.

Time and time again the words of Jesus demonstrated

his Father's commitment to honour the faith of his children.

To a haemorrhaging woman, he said, 'Daughter, your faith has healed you. Go in peace' (Luke 8:47).

To frightened disciples in a raging storm, he asked, 'Where is your faith?' (Luke 8:25).

To blind Bartimaeus, he said, 'Your faith has healed you' (Mark 10:52).

And of Nazareth, his home town, we read, 'He did not do many miracles there because of their lack of faith' (Matthew 13:58).

For his disciples, Jesus had these special words of encouragement:

> Believe me when I say that I am in the Father and the Father is in me; or at least believe on the evidence of the miracles themselves. I tell you the truth, anyone who has faith in me will do what I have been doing. He will do even greater things than these, because I am going to the Father. And I will do whatever you ask in my name, so that the Son may bring glory to the Father. You may ask me for anything in my name, and I will do it.
>
> *John 14:11–14*

Those words put it into a nutshell. Faith in God produces concrete results.

But—why then have so many Christians faced disillusionment, confusion, and a sense of betrayal when they have asked God for specific things and nothing has happened? After all, Jesus did say to a man with a son who was possessed by an epileptic spirit that, 'Everything is possible for him who believes' (Mark 9:23).

In the light of Jesus' specific comments that whenever two of his people were agreed together they could make a request in his name and it would be granted, it seems absolutely inconsistent that often this has not happened.

Following the disciples' open-faced amazement that the fig-tree which he had cursed was now withered, Jesus was quick to encourage them to 'Have faith in God.' He added,

> I tell you the truth, if anyone says to this mountain, 'Go throw yourself into the sea,' and does not doubt in his heart, but believes that what he says will happen, it will be done for him. Therefore I tell you, whatever you ask for in prayer, believe that you have received it, and it will be yours.
>
> *Mark 11:22–24*

Faith, then, is the guarantee that God will act. But . . .

Why then does nothing happen?

When we honestly face up to that question a number of answers emerge. All of them are linked with our failure to live by the standards which God has for us.

(a) Failing to hope

In the past, one of the major dampers on my prayer life was the fact that I didn't really expect God to answer. Even though my conversion was years earlier, I had never really built up a dynamic prayer relationship with God. My prayers were dull and dutiful, if indeed I prayed at all. I occasionally bumped into Christians who frequently claimed all kinds of spectacular answers to prayer, but many of them seemed unbalanced and I didn't want to become like them. I don't think I met too many people upon whose prayer lives I could model my own. The reason for including my testimony here is that so many Christians are in the same rut as I was.

If we take the New Testament as our guide, it is obvious that in those days many people had a remarkably high level of expectation of what God would do. If we felt half as confident as they did, there would be no excuse for stagnant prayer lives. Take, for example, two of the characters in Matthew 9. Both Jairus, who accepted without question that if Jesus merely touched the dead body of his daughter she would be healed, and the haemorrhaging woman, who knew she only had to touch the hem of Jesus' cloak, saw healing—instantly!

The devastating decline in church attendance has resulted in a crippling loss of morale among the people of God. In many cases we have stopped believing that any good can come within our generation—we have run out of hope.

(b) Failing to accept ourselves

The words of Jesus which instruct us to love our neighbours as much as we do ourselves have condemned our neighbours to a very meagre degree of support from the majority of God's people!

So often we judge our own worth by comparison with others—and draw the worst possible conclusions about ourselves. This chronic lack of self-esteem has led many to believe that God would never even dream of using us—after all we're just not suitable!

Yet the living God has created us and he cannot make mistakes and remain God. It is not in his character as the perfect Creator to produce a useless creature. As we see this truth, that God values us and longs to work out his own purposes within our lives, so we will begin to realize that God can, and will, use us!

(c) Failing to perceive faith as God's gift

Often we feel that faith is something which we must manufacture for ourselves, but that is not the case. As the writer of the epistle to the Hebrews reminds us, 'Now faith is being sure of what we hope for and certain of what we do not see' (Hebrews 11:1).

That is a total impossibility for mankind.

He recites a list of heroes in faith: Abraham, Isaac, Jacob, Joseph, Moses' parents, then Moses, Israel,

Gideon, Barak, Samson, Jephthah, David, Samuel—even Rahab, and she was a prostitute! They all exercised faith which was beyond human accomplishment and were commended for it. But we are assured, 'God had planned something better for us' (Hebrews 11:40).

Not only is God's provision of faith open to us, but we have the Holy Spirit within us who brings us the gift of faith. We do not have to summon up our own resources to trust God. In simplicity of devotion we surrender our lives into his hands and allow Jesus to live out his own life within us.

Some years ago, my oldest child Victoria, about eighteen months of age, was standing in her play-pen, with her little chin poking over the top, screaming at the top of her voice. When I walked into the room she continued, but when I picked her up suddenly silence descended while she gave Daddy a great big hug! The Lord came very close and whispered, 'Son if you stop trying to serve me and relax in my arms and do what I tell you, then I can provide all you need.'

So it is with our lack of faith. As the man said, 'I do believe: help me overcome my unbelief' (Mark 9:24).

(d) Failing to forgive

Damage in our relationships with fellow-Christians has resulted in a bitter harvest. Jesus commented on this immediately after his encouraging words that faith can remove mountains. He urged his disciples, 'And when you stand praying, if you hold anything against anyone, forgive him, so that your Father in heaven may forgive you your sins' (Mark 11:25).

Those same insecurities which have made us build up feelings of uselessness, cause us to lash out and seek to destroy one another. God will not fully bless us until we repent of those wrong attitudes and seek forgiveness from him—and from each other.

*(e) Failing to discipline ourselves to fulfil the basic
    spiritual requirements*

Jesus had to rebuke his disciples on this score: 'This kind
can come out only by prayer' (Mark 9:29). Some of the
early source manuscripts add to this verse 'and fasting'.

We have to be prepared to see faith as an expensive
business—requiring our sacrifice of time, energy, and
commitment.

How do we move mountains?

If we are to experience victory in spiritual warfare we
must abandon defeated prayer lives.

Now there is a big difference between 'faith' and
'foolishness'. It is mere foolishness to expect God to
honour and agree to all our own ideas. Faith is understanding the will of God and having unshakeable confidence that, against all odds, he will bring his purposes to
pass.

Nowadays some of us fail to see our prayers answered
in the positive because we pray as we think best and then
for safety's sake add, 'If it be the Lord's will.' James
demanded that in all our planning for the future we acknowledge our dependence on God and say, 'If it is the
Lord's will' (James 4:15), but adds, 'Is any one of you
sick? He should call the elders of the church to pray over
him and anoint him with oil in the name of the Lord.
And the prayer offered in faith will make the sick person
well' (James 5:14–15). The implication is that we will
seek to ascertain the will and purpose of God before we
pray, not afterwards! Otherwise all we are doing is
sweeping all unanswered prayer conveniently under the
carpet (which for some of us could represent ninety per
cent of our specific prayer requests!).

Why did Jesus get positive answers? 'Father, I thank
you that you have heard me. I knew that you always hear

me' (John 11:41–42). A stupendous claim, immediately supported by the resurrection of Lazarus from the dead. Jesus' secret was quite straightforward. He lived so close to his Father that he always knew the will of God *before* he prayed!

The same can be true for believers today. We listen for God's will and then obediently pray along those lines. Jesus said, 'You may ask me for anything in my name, and I will do it' (John 14:14).

The fact is that 'blind faith' is really not blind at all. People like your evangelist friend are building their lives on the plain facts of God's promises. They are not building their hopes on a system or a formula but on the clear manner in which they have seen God at work in the past. That in turn provides them with hope for the future.

I suppose that we all remember initial answers to prayer. Occasions when we first saw faith at work. Sometimes God places us in situations where we cannot follow any other reasonable course of action than to trust him. Scripture and consistent Christian testimony through church history assure us that God is faithful to his people, so out we go on a limb, and then watch his gracious response to our very small faith. As a result our faith gets bigger.

To some God has given the gift of faith in a special way, but to all of us God has entrusted the grace to look up at him, as a child to his or her Father, to place our hand in his and to watch him work wonders.

The story is told of an orphanage in Japan where a group of children knew that an extension was needed for the building and so they prayed. But the only possible site for the extension was occupied by a great hill. However, the children had read, 'I tell you the truth, if anyone says to this mountain, "Go throw yourself into the sea," and does not doubt in his heart, but believes that what he says will happen, it will be done for him. Therefore, I tell you, whatever you ask for in prayer, believe that you have received it, and it will be yours' (Mark 11:23–24). So when they were away on holiday for a fortnight they prayed for the mountain to be put into the sea, and when they returned it had! The local council had decided to reclaim land from the sea. Needing soil as the foundation for a warehouse, they levelled the hill! The need is not for 'big faith' but to recognize a 'big God'.

You may never see something quite like that, but I'll listen with interest to hear the news of the completion of the church centre!

It is significant to note how easily the disciples trusted Jesus. They learned out of three years in close contact with him that his Father answered prayer.

John loved Jesus, and out of that relationship he learned enough to be able to write, 'This is the assurance we have in approaching God: that if we ask anything according to his will, he hears us. And if we know that he hears us—whatever we ask—we know that we have what we asked of him' (1 John 5:14–15).

Although *we* do the praying, it is actually God who initiates prayer. We respond by interceding according to what God has revealed to us. This is quite different to the usual practice of diving in and praying haphazardly for anything which comes into our heads. What I am trying to get across is this—we shall first pray what to pray about unless God's word has already told us—and then get on with it.

But as in every situation with the Lord, there are exceptions to the rule! Sometimes God takes us by surprise and an immediate response is required. A few years ago I was touring across Canada with a Christian music group. We were in two large vans. We had preaching engagements in all the major cities, but often had to drive through the night to get from one place to the next.

One night I was travelling in the second van, trailing the first one, on a long open road. The miles slipped by. Then suddenly the night lit up with a flash! I was sitting in the front passenger seat, next to the driver and gained a grandstand view of all that followed.

The fuel-pipe in the forward van had fractured and petrol was spilling on to the road. The pipe itself had fallen downwards and was now being dragged along the road lighting up the night with the sparks it created. In the following vehicle we knew that the other van had a full tank of petrol and that our friends, both married men, were a second away from eternity. We prayed urgently while our driver desperately tried to gain the attention of the other vehicle, flashing his lights over and over again because he discovered that his horn was out of order. More and more petrol gushed on to the road and into the sparks. Still we prayed.

It seemed an eternity, it must have been all of a minute, before we persuaded the van ahead to stop. When the friends in it got out and saw what had happened they instantly dived into the ditch at the roadside.

It will be no surprise for you to discover that we held a prayer-time of thanksgiving that night for the way in which the living God had reversed the natural order of things for just a few minutes in order to deliver his people from disaster and death. The fact that God answers prayer is never something which we are at liberty to take for granted. Always we should return to say 'thank you'. Such gratitude will rarely be demure, polite and low-key, 'One of them, when he saw he was healed, came back praising God in a *loud voice*. He threw himself at Jesus' feet and thanked him' (Luke 17:15–16, italics mine). It's a real pity about the other nine who never had time to turn their petitions into the release of thanks!

How do we live by faith?

Sometimes I believe that we take it all too casually. We use the words 'If it be the Lord's will' as a spiritual escape route so that we can justify general, rather than specific prayer. That way we avoid taking risks!

Early in our married lives God placed my wife and me in a situation that broke through that barrier. I had gone off to minister in Tyneside, we weren't on the phone at home, and I had not realized that there was no money in the bank (and certainly no overdraft arrangement)! My wife was at home with ten pence in her purse, almost no food in the larder and I was not due back for ten days.

She simply turned to prayer. She had to. There was no room for escape routes. She simply asked God to provide for her and went to bed confident that a cheque would arrive from somewhere in the morning's post. Next morning, no cheque. Nor the next, nor next. Nine mornings came and went before the Lord allowed a cheque to come through! But each day, without her mentioning her needs to anyone, she received all she needed. Transport to and from college, invitations to meals, food on the doorstep, as God demonstrated in a very simple way that specific prayer brings a specific answer! Not necessarily the answer we would have made, but certainly his! Ten days later my wife still had her ten pence, but she also had a story to tell of a Father who loves to answer the prayers of his children.

I believe that we need to recover an understanding of strategic faith in prayer. If we pinpoint that which we believe God is prompting us towards and then pray specifically we will see so much more happen!

Take, for example, the manner in which we pray for non-Christian friends and neighbours. Instead of generally interceding for their conversion, we could translate that sincere desire into a specific plan of action. James reminds us that 'faith without deeds is useless' (James 2:20). He goes on to emphasize that faith and works walked hand in hand in the life of Abraham. 'You see that his faith and his actions were working together, and his faith was made complete by what he did' (James 2:22).

Instead of a vague prayer, in the hope that God will take action, we need to take heed to the advice that we should offer ourselves to be the vehicle for the answer of our own prayer. We need to be available for God to use us to fulfil the needs of those for whom we are praying.

Perhaps the first question to ask about a friend or neighbour is whether or not the Lord wants prayer and faith concentrated on them. If the answer is positive, then ask what your faith can reach to. A possible sequence of events like this could follow:

1. The best you can believe is that your neighbour might talk about Jesus.
2. You pray for that conversation to happen.
3. You make yourself available.
4. When it does, move on to pray for a deeper opportunity. To talk further, to pass on Christian literature or a Bible, to go together to a Christian event, to share in acts of kindness, to be involved socially. Perhaps, subsequently, to lead him to Jesus Christ.

If we recognize that with God nothing is impossible, that God and you are an invincible minority, then truly mountains will move—and the sky is the limit! You see, that's the kind of power that God has made available to ordinary believers like you and me.

Doubters in dog-collars

There is perhaps nothing more sad than to witness sincere and generous men whose years of intellectual study has eroded their faith until little remains. It is more important to be aware that the vast majority of evangelical clergy, elders and leaders are sincere, Bible-believing men and women who are totally committed to moving out in faith for all that God could, and would, do among them.

It is a painful commentary on the times, and perhaps the discrimination of the media, that so much time is given to the disillusioned and the doubting. There has been a grave miscarriage of justice in the way that evangelicals (who make up getting on for half of the Protestant churches and fellowships in this country) have been denied their right to speak with conviction and to renounce the carping doubts of some media-orientated clerics.

No greater harm has been done to the church than wounds inflicted from within. We have misled our secular society with doubts, when only certainties would be attractive. Now many non-Christians believe that we are as confused as themselves!

A statement of faith is not just a set of minimum propositions to which Christians can assent. It is a clarification of the lowest common denominator which a group of Christians regard as essential for spiritual well-being. It is an analysis of those things about which we are confident—and it is those which a dying world needs to appropriate. Not our fears, they have enough of their own.

One afternoon last summer I was on a deserted beach doing some last minute preparation for a series of conference talks. My wife and the children were playing on the other side of this quiet cove. Suddenly our eight-year-old girl Vicky came rushing over, 'Daddy, Daddy, come quickly.' I went over to discover that Vicky had seen our six-month-old baby Suzy playing near a 'golden worm'. She drew my wife's attention to this beautiful little adder six or seven feet from the baby playing happily with the sand. Grabbing the only weapon in sight, a plastic spade, my wife beat the snake to pulp!

It's no good feeling sorry for the snake! It could have killed the baby!

However charitable or courteous we may wish to be towards other churchmen, unbelief is a heinous sin when foisted on new believers and non-Christians. The world is waiting for the positive message of faith which works; it's time we began to proclaim it with confidence!

Now faith needs to be coupled with two things: humility and courage. Humility which gives God *all* the glory, not just part of it! Courage to walk out with him, to stand against unbelief, which is the fashion of the age, and to move in confidence after clearly committing it all to the Lord. Who knows, perhaps one day your name will be added to God's 'Hall of faith', and one day you'll meet them all:

> I do not have time to tell about Gideon, Barak, Samson, Jephthah, David, Samuel and the prophets, who through faith conquered kingdoms, administered justice, and gained what was promised; who shut the mouths of lions, quenched the fury of the flames, and escaped the edge of the sword; whose weakness was turned to strength; and who became powerful in battle and routed foreign armies. Women received back their dead, raised to life again. Others were tortured and refused to be released, so that they might gain a better resurrection. Some faced jeers and flogging, while still others were chained and put in prison. They were stoned; they were sawed in two; they were put to death by the sword. They went about in sheepskins and goatskins, destitute, persecuted and ill-treated—the world was not worthy of them.
>
> *Hebrews 11:32–38*

The world wasn't worthy of them, but they were all commended for their faith. Not for being themselves, but for having the *faith* to allow God to fulfil his purposes in their lives, whatever the cost.

11

The Question Why

It was so strange to see you on the platform last week. Sarah and I only decided to go at the last minute and we had no idea who would be speaking. Imagine my surprise when it turned out to be you! Then my embarrassment because I haven't been in touch for so many months.

As I had told you things have been going really well. It seems almost impossible to believe that I've been a Christian for more than two years! You must have had your share of surprise when you met Sarah, I don't think I've written since we began to go out together.

She's much older as a Christian than I am, having been converted as a teenager. She was brought up in a Christian family and I find a tremendous amount of help and support from her. In fact talking about our faith and praying together has been a real high point for us both.

Don't worry. I've not suddenly become a spiritual giant, it's just that a lot more has been getting together and I think Sarah's had her part to play in that.

I've missed out in not writing and as Sarah and I have a particular problem I wondered if I'd enough nerve to ask if you would be prepared to put pen to paper one more time.

It's just that there is an issue which we've talked about several times but somehow can't arrive at any conclusions.

I think we just need greater understanding on the subject so I suggested that I'd ask for an appropriate essay on the issue—but I warn you—it is a hard one!

Sarah's had a steady relationship with a Christian before, in fact, they were engaged, but he died in a motorcycle accident and she's found it incredibly difficult to understand or accept this. It's funny that time doesn't seem to heal that kind of confusion.

It was a few years ago and I think she's over the emotional loss, only it leaves her with an intellectual problem. Just one big question mark—why did God let it happen? Why does he seem to lose!

This issue is one that defies easy answers. Nobody can give a glib reply, so I'd like to just write in general terms and hope that you and Sarah get to see some light at the end of the tunnel as you read and talk together. Certainly being open and honest about the matter is the most helpful thing you can do—even if the result is for you, as for so many of us, to still ask the question, why?

A close friend of mine provides a very painful illustration.

Twenty past eleven at night and just three miles to go. The glamour which some may ascribe to so-called 'full-time' Christian service lay some hours behind. True, it had been a good meeting. God had been there, speaking through him. Something about the students at Moorlands—they usually wanted to listen; today had been no exception.

He was driving carefully, after all he'd been on the road for nearly three hours. But then, he usually was particular in his driving skills. Most friends said, 'If you want to get there last go with Dave.' Safety conscious, let the lifestyle back up the ministry!

The next thirty seconds will be indelibly imprinted on his memory for life. Two women walked in front of the car. He left their mangled bodies prostrate on the road. The car shuddered to a halt. He walked back to face a living nightmare.

The question . . . why?

Is it God who creates natural disasters? Does he introduce suffering and sickness? Why does God allow decline in his church and disaster for his people?

One of the most powerful attacks on Christians from non-Christians centres on why God allows those who know and love him to suffer.

Often attacks on God's own people crystallize the problem. If God is God, then why doesn't he intervene to deal with things? Why do God's people suffer?

Sandra was a student at Moorlands Bible College. She was tall, slim and extremely attractive. She was a model of all that a Christian young person should be. She studied hard, had many friends and served God whole-heartedly. During the early winter in her first year she began to suffer from backache. It wasn't severe but it troubled her. An appointment was made for her to see a specialist during the vacation. Towards the end of term she felt a little better and decided not to see the specialist. However, I advised her to keep the appointment just to make sure all was well.

The surgeon decided to give her some tests and admitted her to hospital for a few days. I heard nothing more until the middle of the vacation, when I received a phone call to say that she'd had a relapse and was sinking fast. Within two weeks that lovely eighteen-year-old was dead and I had the awful task of breaking the news to the students on the first day of the new term. We were all shattered—not just because she was dead but because it was so unexpected, so undeserved, so unfair. 'Why Sandra?' we asked ourselves.

There was no reason for her to die—she had been such a faithful, hard-working Christian.

This must be a parallel to the death of Sarah's fiancé. And at first sight it throws up far more queries than answers.

Questions like this are crucial. We can never give a complete answer in a few lines but three factors *must* be taken into consideration.

(a) Danger, enemy at work

Anyone who believes that Satan is a sheep in wolf's clothing needs to have their head examined. Every time I have observed the work of Satan at close quarters I have seen nothing but the handiwork of an evil, mal-evolent entity.

(b) Caution, it's not all as it seems

Often the whole truth in a situation is not readily appar-ent. Like an iceberg, seven eighths of the truth lies be-neath the surface where God can view it but we cannot.

(c) Advance, blessing comes from suffering

Painful as an experience can be, it may be the precursor of real blessing. God uses hard times to mature us and in a very real sense we must be careful not to waste our sufferings.

The synchronization of these factors may be as fol-lows: Satan viciously attacks with evil intent. God ascer-tains facts of which we are unaware and turns tragedy into triumph—though not necessarily without personal pain and loss in the process. But that pain is rarely from God—loss and hurt are usually the province of an enemy!

No throw-away pain!

The facts of the matter are different for Christian and atheist. For the latter, this present world is all there is; for the Christian, life on earth is only the prologue to eternity.

How we will spend that eternity is determined here on earth because God is seeking to shape an eternal companion, a Bride for his son, who will reign as co-regent in heaven for eternity.

Now we know that we are in no way fitted for the task. But much as our lack of worth shouts defeat to us, we must remember that Jesus Christ has died to cleanse and restore us, and that Scripture resounds with promises of all that God longs to give us.

The character-shaping which is necessary to prepare us for our eternal role is specified by Paul when he writes, 'If we suffer, we shall also reign with him' (2 Timothy 2:12, AV). He gives a clear outline of the process in these words: 'We also rejoice in our sufferings, because we know that suffering produces perseverance; perseverance, character; and character, hope' (Romans 5:3).

God does not perceive our lives as being worthless or sub-standard. If he did that would be a personal slight on his abilities as our Creator and Redeemer! We are his workmanship but he is still working on us, and suffering is one of his tools.

Michelangelo once patiently chipped away at a fat, ugly block of marble. His painstaking work was mocked by passers-by, particularly when he informed them that an apostle was hidden away in the stone! Yet months later Michelangelo's patience was rewarded: his statue of the apostle Peter still stands in Rome. In the same way, God is chipping away at our lives, moulding them to his likeness, and never demanding more than we are able to give.

H. B. Dehqani-Tafti, Bishop of Iran, suffered incredible things at the end of the nineteen seventies. He just managed to escape assassination. His wife was wounded in saving his life. His only son was murdered, fellow clergy were killed, imprisoned, or forced into exile. Missionary colleagues faced trumped-up charges of spying. This man did not suffer gladly, but he wrote his own personal testimony to the strength which comes from God when his people suffer, and are humble enough to acknowledge their own weaknesses.

> The power to suffer hardship and martyrdom was granted to us by God for each event as it happened, one after another, and we thank him for counting us worthy to witness to his love.
>
> *The Hard Awakening* (Triangle, 1981)

In other words, pain is not just to be rejected and discarded. If God is indeed God, then nothing happens beyond the range of his attention. He can and does ensure that his word is fulfilled and that all things do work together for good.

Suffering saints!

Why then do the righteous suffer?

It has often been argued that hard, self-centred people are not able to face the challenges of Christ's coming kingdom. He calls for a different kind of people to proclaim his love and power.

Such changed lives are not easy to come by. If it is true that 'whole, unbruised, unbroken men are of little use to God', then suffering becomes a means of unanticipated blessing to God's people. Satan would have wished to wreak havoc and unbelief—yet time and again he oversteps the mark and destroys his own objectives.

You may remember that a few years ago I worked for British Youth for Christ. Its chairman, Ron, was a delightful man who had committed many years of his life to the development of that important evangelistic youth ministry. One day while at a staff retreat I received an urgent telephone call. Ron's youngest child had died. It was the school holidays. This fifteen-year-old boy had stayed in bed throughout the morning. At lunchtime his somewhat irate father went upstairs to root him out of bed.

No warning, no illness. He was cold. The family were devastated. But as I tried to murmur words of comfort, I will never forget the reaction of Ron's wife Doreen, 'I don't understand, but I do know that God would only allow this in order that Ian might avoid greater pain and suffering.'

I felt in that moment that I was listening to the expression of an enormously practical faith. A grief-stricken mother could still recognize that a loving God can be trusted, that he knows things we are not even aware of, and nothing is outside of his gaze.

A few days later the coroner's report provided total vindication for the faith of the family. Nobody had known, but Ian had an advanced state of leukaemia. His sufferings could have been considerable—instead he went to sleep one night and never woke up on earth. His journey to heaven was peaceful and painless.

As members of the church of Christ we will one day reign as his Bride. Therefore we are being prepared for that role.

> God's bride-elect is in training for the throne. She is in the school of suffering to learn agape love to qualify her for rulership in an economy where the law of love is supreme. This is why God is willing to take a life time to teach her love.

> Paul Billheimer, *Don't Waste Your Sorrows*
> (Kingsway Publications)

In this way God thwarts Satan's intentions. Far from

destroying faith, God uses suffering as a means by which he can build up and bless his people.

It is significant that throughout the centuries of Christian history it is during periods of persecution that the church has grown most rapidly. The early church historian Tertullian observed that, 'The blood of the martyrs is the seed of the church.' It is still the same today. Where God's people face pressure and persecution, that suffering helps to shape and mould their lives. Without suffering the church can easily grow weak, flabby and self-indulgent.

Who's fooling whom?

We have already affirmed that Satan's plots are being frustrated time and time again. We do, however, need to be careful that we don't fall into the trap of making God the author of disease and death—they are Satan's personal property.

Despite the certainty of his ultimate downfall, it is folly to ignore the realities of Satan's powers here on this earth. In the same way that he was allowed to push Job to the absolute limits of endurance so he is allowed to try, test and tempt each person.

He is aptly named 'the prince of this world' (John 14:30) and we live in his personal domain. His tenure is limited and we must not overestimate his power but we should also be careful not to underestimate his evil intent and authority. Even the archangel Michael didn't dare to criticize the devil but hid behind the ultimate authority of God in order to assure himself of victory (Jude 9). In recalling the event Jude does not deny or ridicule Satan, but points beyond to the One who guarantees our security, 'Him who is able to keep you from falling and to present you before his glorious presence without fault and with great joy' (Jude 24).

The fact is that Satan does possess a degree of power in a world that has surrendered itself to his control. That power only reached a brick wall when it met One who could defeat him on his own home ground—death.

God made people, not robots. We have the right to choose. Our choices have fashioned a degenerate world of disease and death. God's love longs to instal an alternative order and that is the reason for the incarnation, life, death and resurrection of Jesus. So the choice is laid out—follow a self-determinative path in this life or follow Jesus, surrendering the authority of your life to him both for now and for eternity.

Then, and only then, can we receive the forgiveness which Jesus died to give us and the authority to live a different kind of life. Satan won't suddenly stop testing and tempting us, but we can share in Jesus' love, suffering, authority and triumph. And we can join with Michael in proclaiming the victory of our God and his Christ: 'Even the archangel Michael, when he was disputing with the devil about the body of Moses, did not dare to bring a slanderous accusation against him, but said, "The Lord rebuke you!"' (Jude 9).

The character of God is revealed in Scripture as one of love and compassion. In fact, Jesus is often pictured in the Gospels as having such deep concern for ordinary people that his heart is wrung with pity. The Greek word in the New Testament actually refers to compassion from the depths of a man. On the other hand, Satan is clearly portrayed as the father of lies and of all that is harmful and evil. This serves to make a nonsense of the constant accusation that God is behind the trouble in the world— Satan is trying to pass the buck for his own misdeeds!

I still don't understand!

God will never train up a man or woman without utterly

mystifying them. Time and again I have to confess that I don't understand what God is doing with my life, but I do trust him to bring to completion what he has begun. After all, three hundred and sixty six times in Scripture God says, 'Don't be afraid,' that's one for every day of the year and an extra one for leap years!

Satan is never going to slip by on God's blind side. Nothing will ever happen to us without Father's knowledge because, 'He who watches over Israel will neither slumber nor sleep' (Psalm 121:4).

Trusting God to work out his own purposes within us is the key to it all. Then we can have the confidence of Job who proclaimed, 'Though he slay me, yet will I hope in him' (Job 13:15).

The manner in which we face up to suffering is all-important. I tend to go through with gritted teeth. Paul wrote, 'Therefore we do not lose heart. . . . For our light and momentary troubles are achieving for us an eternal glory that far outweighs them all' (2 Corinthians 4:16–17). Paul Billheimer confidently asserts from this passage that:

> Character (agape love) is the coin, the legal tender of heaven. Therefore . . . affliction, triumphantly accepted, slays the self-life, delivers one from self-centredness, and frees one to love.
>
> *Don't Waste Your Sorrows* (Kingsway Publications)

A close friend, a leading preacher, who forms with his wife one of the most powerful ministry teams in the country, arrived at a Christian conference looking white and drawn. He was clearly hurting deep inside, yet retained his full trust in the living God. His sixteen-year-old son had just received a diagnosis of cancer. Two years to live was the curt prognosis the couple had been given. Their fellow-leaders joined them to pray at their son's bedside. For six months the doctors were silent on

the subject as they proceeded with the normal chemo-
therapy treatment. Finally they confirmed that ever since
the church leaders prayed no cancer cell had been evi-
dent!

Other friends lost a twenty-one year-old son who died
on an operating table. They cannot speak of him without
tears coming to their eyes. Yet both couples had faith
strengthened and confirmed in these tragic incidents.
God is working through suffering, just as he did in the
life of his Son. 'To this you were called, because Christ
suffered for you, leaving you an example, that you
should follow in his steps' (1 Peter 2:21).

God is preparing his people for unique tasks in our
generation. That preparation involves moulding and
shaping—and that is not without pain.

> All true believers in all ages are the living stones in that
> heavenly Temple, and God is preparing them in His quarry
> down here, amid the noise and tumult of earth, each for his
> place in His temple above. Rugged and shapeless are the
> stones to begin with: no wonder that the blows of the ham-
> mer fall heavily, that the chisel is sharp, and the polishing
> severe before the stones are ready.
>
> A.N. Hodgkin, *Christ in all the Scriptures*

I realize that these thoughts may be utterly useless to
you both. I find it so difficult to share because everything
sounds so neat or trite, and we all know that life just isn't
like that. Yet the fact is that this world is not yet
redeemed. Christ is coming back, but until that day
sorrow will play its part in the affairs of this world.

The encouragement which I do feel is not just that one
day I will understand, but rather that I'm not left here to
cope alone. No one knows more about suffering than
Jesus. He did not only endure physical torture from
mankind but knew rejection from his Father God as he
took our sin on his own crucified body to bring about our
forgiveness and redemption.

What's more, in our darkest hour he's closest to us, working even the worst situation round to bring some blessing from it.

Just when Satan feels he is winning he finds that all he has done is to serve the purposes of God. Just when we feel that we absolutely cannot cope we discover that God has not left us and has always kept his hand on us. Suffering takes on a new aspect when it is placed in the framework of God's eternal purposes and the amazing fact that we have a part to play within them.

> At present we are not what we should be, neither are we what we shall be. But God does not work without a pattern or design. He knows what he is doing. There is nothing accidental about the providences that come into our lives. There is a hand that is guiding and controlling these providences. There is a purpose running through all the events and circumstances. This purpose may not be evident to us, but there is an eye which always watches the pattern. It is God who fashions us.
>
> Paul Billheimer, *Don't Waste Your Sorrows*
> (Kingsway Publications)

If God seeks for character in his people in order that they might reign with him, if that character cannot be developed without pain, then why do we despise God's moulding of our lives?

Two very close friends are medically unable to have children. They have just had their second, and praised God. This child, a little girl, was born blind. I wept when I heard the news and so did many others. But my tears were put into focus when the couple said, 'We grieved for our friends' sorrow on our behalf. But some of the letters we received made it sound as if our little girl had died.'

Don't waste your sorrows.

12

Triumph in the Air

You know it is getting quite annoying how often you can be right about something! We've just had a great thanksgiving in the fellowship because of the way all the money for the Centre arrived. It was quite amazing, and on the very last day too. The church is so excited. It has been a tremendous answer to prayer.

I do feel it's time to say a real thank you for all the help and encouragement that you've given me over the last five years. Your latest essay or letter, as always, arrived right on cue.

Sarah and I had been getting quite serious in our relationship but the queries in her mind kept getting in the way. Your last little treatise on suffering really helped us to talk it all through. It'll take time but we've been to the vicar for prayer and help and the whole thing really seems to be getting sorted out now.

I suppose that leads me on fairly naturally to the next point. You will be receiving an invitation—it's to a wedding! We hope to be getting married in about six months' time and then go on to missionary training because we both feel that God wants us to serve him in another country.

When you've got up from the floor I'll explain more!

I know it will be a surprise to you, but the last few years have been a real growing experience. We don't want to waste our lives and feel that the time at college will confirm God's call to us. Yes, I know Britain needs help and I could serve God properly in a secular profession, but I've been hammered by the Lord to move in this way—so I'm only being obedient!

By the way, I was speaking at the Poly Christian Union (of bitter memory), and there was this guy sitting at the back. We talked through half the night and agreed to meet again to talk further. I think he reminded me of someone! Anyway I wouldn't be at all surprised if he doesn't follow a similar pathway to my own.

I realize I'm rambling on a bit but so many encouraging things are happening. Just one sobering note—in your last treatise you used the words 'whatever the cost'. As you know, I've experienced both failure and joy as a Christian. I would appreciate your 'waxing lyrical' on the subject. Perhaps you'd take the opportunity of summarizing what Christian commitment is all about? Perhaps it'll end up as a synopsis of all that has already passed between us?

You see, I remember Malcolm Muggeridge once talking about 'another King'. I guess that's exactly what Sarah and I have discovered in our lives—now we just want to serve him, whatever the cost.

However I can't help but feel that we're only starting the preparation phase. I feel so unsuitable and so unworthy yet I do sense God's call on my life. I'd really like to be confident that I'll meet the test.

That was certainly an interesting closing comment! So often God makes us face up to the testing situations in order that our true calibre can be determined. The children of Israel faced just such a trial.

But the Israelites acted unfaithfully. . . . Now Joshua sent men from Jericho to Ai, which is near Beth Aven to the east of Bethel, and told them, 'Go up and spy out the region.' So the men went and spied out Ai.

When they returned to Joshua, they said, 'Not all the people will have to go up against Ai. Send two or three thousand men to take it, and do not weary all the people, for only a few men are there.' So about three thousand men went up; but they were routed by the men of Ai, who killed about thirty-six of them. They chased the Israelites from the city gate as far as the stone quarries and struck them down on the slopes. At this the hearts of the people melted and became like water.

Joshua 7:1–5

'But . . . but . . . I thought God always gave victory to his people. I thought they couldn't lose!'

Don't you see they broke their agreement with God by being unfaithful? Then they failed to turn to him for instructions. Defeat was the inevitable result.

History is littered with the names of those who claimed, 'God on our side.' The reason is simple. Alone we fail, but with the support of the living God defeat is impossible. As the Psalmist asserts, 'With God we shall gain the victory' (Psalm 60:12).

Tragically, this concept has been prostituted by self-seekers demanding God's support for their own initiatives. Such manipulation of the divine artillery is not possible. Time and time again those who claimed to have God on their side faced failure and defeat. George Bernard Shaw in *St Joan* cynically observed, 'God is on the side of the big battalions.'

To believe that God has failed because he refuses to bow to our wishes, or to conform to our requirements, is arrant nonsense. It is only as we submit to his agenda for our lives that God fulfils our destiny by giving us a part to play in his plan for the world. We must stop devising our own plans and asking God to bless them. Instead we must be flexible so that God may bring victory to his people by indicating his own initiatives!

David discovered this truth at the Battle of Rephaim. Where God dictates the battle plans (and he employs differing methods) he brings the victory! As we listen and follow so God gives victory.

The Lord answered him, 'Go, for I will surely hand the Philistines over to you.'
So David went to Baal Perazim, and there he defeated them. . . .
Once more the Philistines came up and spread out in the Valley of Rephaim; so David enquired of the Lord, and he answered, 'Do not go straight up, but circle round behind them and attack them in front of the balsam trees. As soon as you hear the sound of marching in the tops of the balsam trees, move quickly, because that will mean the Lord has gone out in front of you to strike the Philistine army.' *So David did as the Lord commanded him*, and he struck down the Philistines all the way from Gibeon to Gezer.
                                    2 Samuel 5:19, 22–25, italics mine

That is the one and only way to know the guaranteed victory of the living God, both in our lives, and in our projects and dreams. In the words of Mary, 'Do whatever he tells you' (John 2:5). Because they did, water became wine, and joy continued at the wedding feast! If our lives are marked by that kind of obedience then victory becomes a way of life!

It is that kind of trained response which God wants to create within our lives. He wants us to follow his directions, whatever the cost may be. This means that we hand our lives over to the Lord, not merely for direction, but also to put them under his government in order that he may mature and mould us to be the people that he wants us to be. Perhaps it is your sense that God has his hand on your life in that kind of way which has provoked the question? What God is doing in our lives is all summed up in South American pottery!

Peruvian pottery for beginners

The moulded clay is placed in the little oven. The baking is simple, but the trick of the Peruvian potter is to heat that clay to the point when he can remove the pot from the oven and flick its rim with his finger. If the pot sings then it is perfect, if not it goes back into the oven to face the heat until it has reached completion.

God is doing exactly the same with his people. Not because he is a harsh, arbitrary God, but because he longs that we might become all that we could be. What is more, we will never arrive at our full potential until our lives are surrendered to his discipline and have been brought to the point where they 'sing' to the praise of the potter who has moulded us.

What right does God have to do this? If we have surrendered ourselves to him then we have given him the mandate to do as he wants with our lives. 'Does the clay say to the potter, "What are you making?"' (Isaiah 45:9). No, of course not. What's more, if the potter is the Creator God, then we can be convinced that it would deny his character to get it wrong!

As far back as around 2000 BC 'God tested Abraham' (Genesis 22:1). He asked Abraham to murder his only son in brutal child-sacrifice. Once Abraham had proved that he would even obey this demand which contradicted God's own nature, an angel intervened to reveal the true character of God—'Do not lay a hand on the boy' (Genesis 22:12). Now God knew he had a man he could trust. So the promise came, and the Jews have remembered it ever since: 'Because you have done this . . . . I will surely bless you and make your descendants as numerous as the stars in the sky and the sand on the seashore' (Genesis 22:16–17).

Whenever Israel has been faithful to God and obeyed the basic requirements he has laid upon them as his exclusive people, God's blessing has followed them. When Israel has broken the covenant or agreement with God then punishment has been inevitable. But God never gives up his people. He would return to test Israel again to see if she had learned her lesson and would now be faithful.

At one point in their history (around 1400 BC), 'The people returned to ways even more corrupt than those of their fathers, following other gods and serving and worshipping them. They refused to give up their evil practices and stubborn ways' (Judges 2:19). Therefore, God cut off their stream of easy victories and made Israel face bitter conflict with other nations. He announced, 'I will use them to test Israel and see whether they will keep the way of the Lord and walk in it as their forefathers did' (Judges 2:22).

Seven hundred years later, King Hezekiah of Judah was even abandoned by God for a while, 'To test him and know everything that was in his heart' (2 Chronicles 32:31). As Isaiah prophesied from God about Israel's stubbornness: 'I have tested you in the furnace of affliction' (Isaiah 48:10).

What then is the point of this emphasis on testing? God said through Jeremiah, 'See, I will refine and test them, for what else can I do because of the sin of my people?' (Jeremiah 9:7). Some would have gone too far to be brought back, but others could be restored: '"In the whole land," declares the Lord, "two-thirds will be struck down and perish; yet one-third will be left in it. This third I will bring into the fire; I will refine them like silver and test them like gold. They will call on my name and I will answer them"' (Zechariah 13:8–9).

The refiner would heat the gold until the impurities in

it rose to the surface. At that time he could skim them off. Then the heat in the furnace would be increased so that more impurities could rise until in the end the refiner could look into the gold and see his own reflection. That is exactly what Jesus is doing to us in our lives, because he loves us, and longs to bring out the full potential of his love and grace in us.

The process of turning the heat up may sometimes involve suffering. Some may object that if God loves us, we Christians should never suffer. Yet his Son endured unimaginable agonies for us.

As the psalmist writes, 'Before I was afflicted I went astray, but now I obey your word' (Psalm 119:67). When we learn to handle hardships correctly character building will result. Paul even encourages us to 'Rejoice in our sufferings', and then explains the reason for this improbable statement, 'Because we know that suffering produces perseverance; perseverance, character; and character, hope' (Romans 5:3–4). In fact, James is even more emphatic, insisting that we, 'Consider it pure joy . . . because you know that the testing of your faith develops perseverance. Perseverance must finish its work so that you may be more mature and complete, not lacking anything' (James 1:2–4).

Some Christians do manage to develop spiritually in the absence of testing—but most of us don't. It's just the same in the military life. Most soldiers have to learn how to survive under rough, tough conditions. Sometimes they face harsh and cruel treatment. Yet few methods have proved to be equally effective in producing tough, obedient, self-disciplined men and women. God allows his people to endure hardship—not that he might enjoy watching our hurt, but so that he can see us grow into fruitful maturity.

The last thing that God wants us to do is fall back from the pathway he has for us. Because we are his creation he knows us best and therefore wants to equip us for the problem-times in order that we may resist Satan and come through into all that God has for our lives.

Satan is determined to make us take our eyes off the Lord and concentrate on our own weaknesses and failings.

> Then Peter got down out of the boat and walked on the water to Jesus. But when he saw the wind, he was afraid and, beginning to sink, cried out, 'Lord, save me!'
> Immediately Jesus reached out his hand and caught him. 'You of little faith,' he said, 'why did you doubt?'
>
> Matthew 14:29–31

The secret is to stretch out in faith keeping our eyes, heart and faith firmly on Jesus. Then by his strength we'll find we're still standing. Satan's prime attack is reserved for just this point—trying to convince us that we're not standing! This attempt at condemnation is often both insidious and pervasive. We convince ourselves of five things:

(a) I'm useless

God uses people, but he could never use me. So I might as well live life just as it comes.

(b) I'm a failure

Every time I try to get it right, everything is fine for a day or two but then I fail again.

(c) I'm rotten

God could never really forgive me for all that I've done and that I am.

(d) I'm losing

I can't do enough in the present to compensate for all the

negatives in the past.

(e) I'm inferior

I don't come up to the standards of other Christians. I set higher and higher ones for myself, and end up continuing to condemn myself for failing to reach my own standards.

Just when we think we're getting along fine because we're succeeding in avoiding obvious areas of sinful conduct, Satan tries to draw us into self-condemnation and doubt. He knows that if he can keep your eyes fixed on yourself, then you and Sarah will never serve the Lord. Constantly we need to recognize that 'There is now no condemnation for those who are in Christ Jesus, because through Christ Jesus the law of the Spirit of life set me free from the law of sin and death' (Romans 8:1–2).

You see when we doubt ourselves we are casting doubt on the creative abilities of Father God and the sufficiency of Christ's death on the cross to provide complete salvation. God has made us gloriously different from each other. This variety destroys the myth that we are only a bunch of evangelical 'Homepride flour-graders' emerging from a divine conveyor belt. Comparisons with other Christians can never be an adequate guide to our growth and development in God. What is more, we are the people God has made us to be. If we are daily surrendering our lives into the arms of Jesus then he is at work changing us into the likeness of himself.

But Christianity is no one-off experience. We must never be too impatient with either ourselves or with others. My family were at a large Christian convention. A special family evening had been arranged but my small children could not see what was happening on the platform. So, being at the back of the hall, they stood up. A teenager behind them let out a storm of abuse. My wife turned to explain the situation and correct his violent over-reaction when her eyes spotted the words on his T-shirt.

'Please have patience. God hasn't finished dealing with me yet.'

That says it all. Satan will seek to tell us that we'll never make it, but by the grace and power of God he will work out his own purposes within our lives in order that we may be suitable soldiers for his army.

God's guerilla group

Just as David trained the nucleus of his army out of an assorted mish-mash of people gathered together at the Caves of Adullam, so Jesus took a handful of men and women and made of them the origins of a force that would turn the world upside down.

There can be no doubt that the early church became an overcoming community. Life was 'a triumphal procession in Christ' (2 Corinthians 2:14).

* They knew exactly where they stood, and so did everyone else.

* They spoke out boldly for all they had discovered in Jesus.

* They were swiftly transformed from a fearful minority group into a powerful influence for God and for good in their society.

* They were so certain of their faith that they faced the gravest risks without flinching.

* They were convinced that the dangers and persecutions were insignificant in comparison with the thrill of going all out for Christ.

Like soldiers belonging to a successful wartime regiment, they never expected the result to be anything but victory. Jesus beckoned them on and they knew that one day they would be accountable to him for their lives and service. Convinced that they could do nothing to earn or deserve salvation, they had a vital personal friendship with the one who had died to give salvation to them. But they knew what it was to live in the light of the judgement seat of Christ. Their hope was that one day he would be able to say to them, 'Well done, good and faithful servant! . . . Come and share your master's happiness!' (Matthew 25:21).

Those early Christians were only too aware that their Commander had already prepared the way for their success through his example, cross, resurrection, ascension, and gift of the Spirit. All they had to do was respond to his leadership in the fight against Satan and the forces of darkness.

Their understanding of doctrine was probably much less complicated than ours today. Few would have passed an 'O' level in New Testament theology. But they knew sufficient about the things that really mattered. Power, love, and provision were not merely concepts to be studied and analysed—they were living realities.

The message which they communicated to the pagan world carried power, conviction and authority because they did not just speak it out, they lived it!

* Their single-minded devotion to Christ resulted in a remarkable unity of attitude and action.

* Their bodies became human torches in Nero's gardens, but the early church historian Tertullian reported, 'The blood of the martyrs is the seed of the church.'

* Their enemies, inside and out, tried to wipe them out and failed.

* Their lifestyle was such that they praised God and served each other regardless of personal cost.

* Their lives were lived under the microscope of public investigation and thousands were converted!

Perhaps because of their very simplicity, perhaps because of their readiness to believe, to obey, to give, to suffer, and if need be to die, the Spirit of God found what he must always be seeking—a fellowship of men and women so united by love and faith that He can work in them and through them with the minimum of hindrance.

J.B. Phillips, Introduction to Acts,
The New Testament in Modern English (Macmillan)

Thankfully, a growing number of churches do resemble the triumphant early church. Regrettably, many still suffer from deadness, pessimism, apathy and defeat. Some are painfully aware of the problem but they have no idea of how to get out of the rut. Other churches are even worse off—they are spiritually at a low ebb but don't even recognize that anything is wrong.

The church is only composed of individuals like you and me. It is here that change must begin: we must become part of the answer, instead of being part of the problem; not going back to the problems of a couple of years ago, but moving on to show that now victory has replaced defeat.

The roots of the difficulty lie in the fact that instead of waking up in the morning with an eager anticipation of all that God might do during the day, many individuals display a low sense of expectancy. There is no real appetite for prayer and Bible meditation. Some have too little self-discipline even to make the effort. It becomes a vicious circle—the less they feel inclined, the less effort they make. That in turn robs God of the opportunity to speak to them.

Where the rubber hits the road

The level of commitment of many to both God and their fellow Christians is far too low. Their priorities are wrong. Too small a proportion of their resources, love, time, homes and money are allocated to God. A number are so embroiled in 'the world' that they adopt attitudes which are out of keeping with New Testament teaching (Romans 12:2). They have a low or even sceptical view of the 'crucified life', which in their opinion is far too intense. To them, rugged and costly obedience is seen as an optional extra for the kind of people who are suited to it. On the whole, Christians today have swung from the heavy legalism of the past to a rather easy going lifestyle with the excuse that, 'God has given us everything for our enjoyment', or, 'Non-Christians need to see that I'm normal'. If anything, such Christians may need to cease pampering themselves and turn to a more realistic and more biblical view of the Christian life. I believe that's why you've asked the question, and I want to be equally honest about the answer.

God never intended that the difference between a Christian and non-Christian lifestyle should boil down to minor habits or slightly different cultural activities. Instead, God wants those who bear his name to be so different in the way we treat other people and the way we live ourselves that nobody can miss the difference.

What is more, that difference should also apply to the way we regard the enemy. It was that great Pentecostal pioneer Smith Wigglesworth who woke one morning to recognize Satan standing at the foot of his bed. Now he knew two great truths. He was a defeated sinner who was forgiven and he was covered by the blood of Jesus. His response is a textbook illustration for all who would seek to live the victorious Christian life. He transplanted objective truth into subjective experience. Looking at Satan he said, 'Oh, it's only you,' turned over and went to sleep!

You see, our Christian activities, be they preaching or playing a vital role in the church, are never enough. Our lives must be the living evidence of the truth of our words. For many of us this will require a growth in self-discipline, which normally will be far from easy. Only then will we be able to echo the words of Paul, 'I do not fight like a man beating the air. No, I beat my body and make it my slave so that after I have preached to others, I myself will not be disqualified for the prize' (1 Corinthians 9:26–27).

Nowadays there is no shortage of plausible excuses why this emphasis should be regarded as old-fashioned or out of date.

(a) Some of us are lazy and can't really be bothered.

(b) Some believe that victory in God is automatic; all we have to do is sit back and wait.

(c) Others wear themselves out in personal self-examination or analysis of the quality of worship and ministry in the local church.

(d) Still others hesitate to get involved for fear that the Holy Spirit might become more in fact than they can accept in theory!

So we settle down into a way of self-satisfied evangelical comfort. We dig in for safety and seek to conserve our gains.

God sometimes surprises us with unexpected successes even when there's been no effort on our part, but on the whole most things don't happen automatically. For example, the stifling of the power of our old nature rarely happens by itself. That inner urge to pray may never come. We won't normally experience the fruit of the Spirit without doing something consciously to bring it about. Finally, battles don't fight themselves.

The early church seemed to be composed of outward-looking individuals who had a great sense of adventure. They were so generously disposed towards others that they rarely seemed to seek anything for themselves. Today there is unfortunately a good deal of selfishness. Often there is too much preoccupation with airing resentments, too much taking offence over trivial matters, too much wallowing in self pity, in self-justification and too many power struggles—in short, we spend too long thinking about how things affect us rather than how God can use us to radically change an entire situation. Involvement may be costly and uncomfortable, but it is absolutely essential if things are to change. If we all opt out of responsibility, then nothing will ever be different.

Sadly, what we have described is fairly commonplace. No wonder there are few overcomers around; we're all concentrating on bare survival!

He never promised you a rose garden

Society today offers the 'new' and 'instant'. Jesus' kingdom is 'new' but its establishment in our lives represents an ongoing process. When Jesus taught his disciples to pray he used typical Hebrew parallelism. In other words, the same thing is said twice:

> Your kingdom come,
> Your will be done
>   on earth as it is in heaven
> *Matthew 6:10*

So the kingdom of Jesus is established in our lives at the time when we have a set policy of following his will rather than our own. Simply, we abdicate the throne in our own lives and allow Jesus to reign there instead. As a friend of mine puts it so succinctly, 'I know you know this, I only wanted to remind you.'

Self-discipline is not very popular today. The Olympics amply illustrate that an athlete isn't likely to win if he eats too much, sleeps too much (or too little) and lazes around. The Christian who refuses to focus only on what matters will not enjoy victory. Whatever hinders us must be eradicated ruthlessly, whether it's 'worldly' entanglements, wrong priorities or getting bogged down in trivial details of church life. We all have trouble with sin and self, and the crucifying of self can be very painful. As Paul said, 'I beat my body, and make it my slave' (1 Corinthians 9:27). No one enjoys doing that because we all have an inborn resistance to being beaten!

There's nothing quite like the thrill of winning a race and being publicly acclaimed. Yet ours is not just a human competition for a gold medal in front of a crowd of spectators. Our race is shared by millions in the church under the leadership of a resurrected, victorious Jesus. Even so, the danger is still there that if we concentrate on our weaknesses and failings then defeat is virtually assured.

But hold on a moment. The living God has given us his personal guarantee that he is fighting on our side. What's more, heaven is filled with the saints of God shouting encouragement to us as we run around the arena of life. An even greater inducement is the knowledge that Jesus is at the finishing tape beckoning us on and providing all the strength which we need.

> Therefore, since we are surrounded by such a great cloud of witnesses, let us throw off everything that hinders. . . . Let us fix our eyes on Jesus. . . . Consider him who endured such opposition from sinful men, so that you will not grow weary and lose heart.
>
> *Hebrews 12:1–3*

Yet even with that reassurance it is still not possible for us to will and do all that God requires within our lives in our own strength alone. It is as we surrender our lives into God's arms, as children relaxing into their Father, that we can begin to draw on every resource that his indwelling Spirit gives us. It does take time to learn how to begin but most things can only be done well after training and plenty of practice. Few worthwhile skills are acquired in a day—they take time to develop even in

today's 'instant' society. As the old expression goes—
'Practice makes perfect'.

In order to be victorious in each area of our lives we
need to build up resources from which we can draw day
by day. The most powerful and permanent source of
strength is Christ himself. That's why growth into Christ
is essential. Above all else, that relationship needs to be
nurtured daily—victory ultimately comes through him,
and he is in us and we are in him. Paul writes, 'Clothe
yourselves with the Lord Jesus Christ' (Romans 13:14)
and 'Be strong in the Lord and in his mighty power'
(Ephesians 6:10). The psalmist glories in 'God who arms
me with strength' (Psalm 18:32) by referring to him as
our rock, fortress, deliverer, shield and salvation and
stronghold (Psalm 18:2).

As Paul summarized it, 'Do not conform any longer to
the pattern of this world, but be transformed by the re-
newing of your mind. Then you will be able to test and
approve what God's will is—his good, pleasing and perfect will' (Romans 12:2).

Some Christians think that the power of the Spirit is
only available to make things easier. That is both true
and false. One of his tasks is to equip us for battle. To do
that he needs our co-operation. For his work to be effective we must exercise strict self-discipline—'Everyone
who competes in the games goes into strict training'
(1 Corinthians 9:25). Furthermore, we must be completely open to his activity in our lives. Our own efforts
cannot please God, only his Spirit can reproduce his lifestyle and likeness within us. There comes a time when
each of us realizes that fact and has to turn to the Lord
for an answer from him.

Many people are fearful because of exaggerated ru-
mours and negative teaching about the work of the Holy
Spirit. Some are frightened because one or two of their
friends have 'gone overboard' on the Holy Spirit. We

mustn't be dominated by fears and bad experiences. We must rely instead on what God is saying to us through the Bible—that's the surest way of knowing what's right and wrong.

Now Scripture is quite straightforward on this issue. All believers need to be filled with the Holy Spirit. That alone is our safeguard against living in the flesh. What is more this is no 'one-off' experience. When Paul told the Ephesians to 'be filled with the Spirit' (Ephesians 5:18), the Greek word he used is more properly translated 'continue to be being filled'. In other words, far from being afraid of the Holy Spirit, we need to be filled with him every moment of the day. But we have to start somewhere, and that place is before the Lord in total surrender, asking for his power to live our lives for him.

Now Scripture is not definitive about how this all begins. It is clear that the moment we give our lives to Jesus Christ his Spirit indwells us. However, we often limit or shackle his activity in our lives. Whether it is a crisis baptism, a release, or a filling that breaks the dam obstructing the Holy Spirit's work, or whether the barrier is steadily pierced by progressive sanctification—how it happens is not the most important issue. God employed a glorious variety in creation. We, as his people are each unique and so is the way in which he deals with our lives. It is the end result which is all important. That result is that our lives should be filled with the Holy Spirit so that Jesus is glorified and seen in each one of us! Above all, we must know the reality of the power of God at work in our lives and for that we must first turn to him.

My writing was interrupted last week by an attractive woman of twenty-six who came to see me in my study. She was a clean-living, hard-working, godly Christian, yet she was spiritually dry and had been throughout her Christian life. Her prayer times were a constant battle, the Bible rarely came alive, though she read it faithfully, and she had no joy or motivation in her service in the church. She was just about ready to give up and yet somehow she knew she mustn't, because God had saved her. There had to be an answer to it all. Like me, she had been taught to ignore the Holy Spirit, but as the years went by she began to notice with envy that there were those whose lives appeared to be both rich and free. She eventually realized that the ingredient in their lives which was missing in hers was the fullness and power of the Spirit. Despite all her efforts, she knew she was getting nowhere and she desperately wanted her life to be different. Her determination to be changed gave her the courage to seek help. That afternoon we prayed together that God would transform her life by filling her with the Spirit as she yielded her life to his control.

Getting your head down—overcomers united

Christianity is plagued by extremism. No sooner have we discovered truth from God than we try to place it in a humanly understandable framework, usually by trying to push that truth so far that it becomes totally distorted! No sooner have we recognized that the Christian life is to be lived in a Father's loving arms and empowered by his Spirit than we expect it to be a bed of roses—forgetting the thorns!

We have no right to expect to retire from the place of battle. Our Christian life isn't going to be a quiet, restful experience while God gets on with the battle. He expects us to put our heads down in a very different way! When everything seems to be going wrong he longs that we might not give up, but keep on going trusting him to bring us through in the end.

Unfortunately, today there are too many Christians who have been misled into thinking that victory comes on a plate. They rather resemble that small proportion of the unemployed who are not prepared to make the slightest effort to look for work—they simply sit around waiting for a job to land on their lap. Such Christians somehow expect guidance to drop out of heaven. They don't pray unless they feel the urge. Some are unable to make the simplest decisions in life because they have ceased using their God-given intellect and powers of reasoning. They are totally passive—as limp and lifeless as a hot air balloon when the burners are turned off.

Such passivity makes people gullible—easily influenced, subject to extreme 'highs' and 'lows'. They have taken the 'Let go and let God' concept too far.

Paul is quick to stress the need to persevere, using expressions like 'I press on', 'I labour', and 'Straining towards what is ahead' (Philippians 3:14, Colossians 1:29, Philippians 3:13). Paul knew that only the power of God gives strength to conquer, and that God takes and uses ordinary people who trust him.

Satan is quick to try to make us believe that he is no longer active. Quick also to tempt us to become introverted, preoccupied with ourselves and ignorant of God's purposes for our lives.

Here lies a grave danger. In discovering God's desire to meet us in the areas of our personal needs we have lost sight of the importance of sharing his love with others. As we have concentrated on recovering self-esteem, self-love, acceptance, security and 'job satisfaction' we have assumed that we must find a way to alleviate practically all emotional suffering. The combination of the idea that all our needs must be met, with the secular philosophy that life must come on a plate, has made us vulnerable to the temptation to avoid even God-ordained hardships, struggles, deprivations and pain, which he allows for our own development and for his glory.

These temptations must be resisted, otherwise a few

knocks could prove fatal to our spiritual life. After all, a 'me-centred' mind is an easy target for Satan. He can feed it with many attractive propositions. He can persuade us that committing certain sins may be regarded as legitimate because we have the excuse that we are controlled by our past hurts. Or he could tell us to give in to some temptations on the grounds that God created us with human needs and they must be satisfied at all costs.

Satan has a ready supply of easy excuses and cop-outs for the Christian. These pain-relieving suggestions may always seem to be attractive and God's way can sometimes appear to be cruel by comparison. We must recognize that we are soldiers and that pain, along with hardship, is part of our Christian lives. We will suffer as we resist temptation, just as Jesus did.

When we suspect we are being tempted, we must avoid dwelling on it with our minds because it will get more and more appealing. We can ask ourselves some basic questions like, 'Is this a need or a want?' 'Is the idea from God or Satan?' Is the temptation similar to one of the temptations that Jesus faced in the wilderness—is it an illegitimate satisfaction of bodily need, a desire for false security or a short cut? If it is a real need, then we may enquire, 'Is what I'm thinking of doing, God's provision for that need?' Once we conclude that a proposition is from Satan, we must cease mulling it over and focus on something completely different.

On every occasion we must be careful to follow what our conscience dictates as the right course rather than being swayed by personal feelings. Fortunately we have not been left alone in this situation. Help is near at hand. We are surrounded by thousands of brothers and sisters. After all, isn't that where you and I have been at over the years? We may often need the help of a pastor, an elder, or a trusted Christian friend in order to withstand some particular temptation.

Basing our actions on biblical facts and commands is really the same as using the shield of faith (Ephesians 6:16) because it means we believe that God knows what is best for us.

If we were faced with the task of having to blaze a trail for ourselves it would all be too much for us to cope with. Left to ourselves we cannot win. But Jesus has captured the ground for us and in his victory we can take complete confidence. We need to be reminded, as Peter was, that Jesus has not left us alone but has given us the gift of his Spirit. What's more, he is personally praying for us.

Even with the help of the Overcomer, we cannot simply sit back and let God do all the work. We have a responsibility to make an effort in collaboration with God. The secret of success lies in that combination of human effort and the power of God. As Paul described his Christian life, 'I worked harder than all of them [the Apostles]—yet not I, but the grace of God that was with me' (1 Corinthians 15:10).

The final chapter

Satan is on the run—and he knows it. But he certainly hasn't given up yet. One thing he longs to do is to keep Christians tied up in bondage to their past sinful actions, their sinful nature and legalistic attitude. In that way he can stand over them as their accuser, gloating over their agonized consciences, creating deep inner fears about their acceptability to God. At the same time he persuades Christians slavishly and miserably to follow man-made religious rules and regulations.

Jesus' death, resurrection and ascension took care of all that. As Paul writes in Colossians 2:13–14, 'When you were dead in your sins. . . . He forgave us all our sins, having cancelled the written code . . . that was against us

. . . he took it away, nailing it to the cross.' There are no more grounds for accusation—'Who will bring any charge against those whom God has chosen?' (Romans 8:33).

With the frustration of Satan's last frantic efforts at deception, the book of Revelation depicts the final moments of the coming conflict.

A wild and desperate 'one-hour' battle is described in Revelation 17:12–14. It will be directed against Christ and his followers. Yet John says that the Lamb will win because he is Lord of lords and King of kings, a position of dominion declared to be his at his birth (12:5).

As we move on in the Apocalypse, Satan's chief agents (the beast and the false prophet) plus their massive armies are captured. Christ slaughters all the soldiers, but the two agents are punished by being thrown alive 'into the fiery lake of burning sulphur' (19:19–21).

The last three chapters of Revelation draw God's purposes in history to their inevitable conclusion. The ghastly abyss is unlocked by an angel as a prison for Satan. Further conflict results in his permanent exile, along with the beast and the false prophet, into an awful fiery location!

After this terrible bloodshed and turmoil, everything will become incredibly tranquil and lovely. All forms of suffering will end for ever. All that is distasteful to God will be completely removed. Heaven and earth will be thoroughly cleansed of all traces of Satan and his activities. The thousands of years of Satan's harassment will be over. Instead, there will be eternal life and light, with God and his people reigning for ever (22:1–5).

This all-triumphant climax of the ministry of Jesus Christ described in Revelation is linked directly with his death, the wounds to his body being specifically mentioned in Revelation 1:7. In the search for someone worthy enough to open the scroll of heaven, one of the elders said, 'Do not weep! See, the Lion of the tribe of

Judah . . . has triumphed. He is able to open the scroll
and its seven seals' (5:5). Yet when that great personage
actually steps forward it is a 'Lamb, looking as if it had
been slain' (5:6)—not the expected mighty Lion, but one
who had been crucified. And in 12:11, those who
overcome the Accuser did so, 'by the blood of the
Lamb'.

Preparing for the throne

As we receive the promise that one day we will reign with
Jesus Christ in heaven we should learn to live increasingly in his victory here on earth. These are lessons which
keep us confident in whatever situation we find ourselves. After all four things are secure.

(a) Ultimate victory has been secured.

(b) We don't need to rely on our own strength. Indeed, that would be a fatal response when the power of
God's Spirit is available.

(c) God's word, promises and presence are all available to us.

(d) Our faith can look into his reality knowing that his
battle is won already!

If we are to share in his success then we ought to be
'self-controlled and alert' (1 Peter 5:8).

Self-confidence and laziness must give way to an
attitude of watchfulness which is our defence against
those unexpected attacks which Satan provides for unsuspecting Christians. At Gethsemane, Jesus both prayed and watched, and he told the disciples to do the same
(Mark 14:34, 38). Even those of us who are helping
others are to be on our guard. 'But watch yourself, or
you also may be tempted' (Galatians 6:1).

The secret of success over temptation hinges on the
way in which God cares and provides for us as his children. We so underestimate his care. We cannot gain our

own victory—but he can, and will do it through us.

A few weeks ago on holiday in Cornwall, my little girl Victoria's bikini bottom was washed out to sea. Scarcely a major tragedy, you may say, but it was vitally important to her. That bikini was a present which I had brought her back from a preaching trip to Guernsey. It was rainbow striped, very trendy and highly popular with Vicky. I had been washing out the family swimming gear when a surprise wave carried the bikini bottom out to sea!

For an hour we swam and searched. Back again we came at night to search once more. The next day, after two tides, and another hour's search there on a rock was the missing swimwear. The thanksgiving meeting on the beach was spontaneous and sincere. Vicky is eight years old and she had believed that God could and would work it out. Her faith was a lesson in victory for us all.

> I pray that out of his glorious riches he may strengthen you with power through his Spirit in your inner being, so that Christ may dwell in your hearts through faith. And I pray that you, being rooted and established in love, may have power, together with all the saints, to grasp how wide and long and high and deep is the love of Christ, and to know this love that surpasses knowledge—that you may be filled to the measure of all the fulness of God.
>
> *Ephesians 3:16–19*

There is a lifestyle which the Spirit of God longs to create among his people. This is no mere stereotype. It is characterized by the fruit which he brings to birth within us. We will never be able to produce spiritual fruit by our own good resolutions or self-effort. Fruit-bearing is always a natural process. After all, when did you last see an apple tree in the middle of an orchard struggling for breath, writhing in agony, and screaming to produce 'apples . . . pips . . . cores'? Yet many Christians seem to be trying to please God by enduring this kind of process!

If an apple tree has sunlight, roots and moisture then it will grow—naturally! In exactly the same way, if we are open to the sunlight of God's love, if we are rooted in our relationship with him through the Bible and prayer, and also relaxing in the fullness of his Spirit—then growth and fruit are the inevitable results.

The problem for so many of us lies in the fact that we are still trying too hard! We suffer from a peculiar vanity which demands that we have to play a significant part in God's divine activities within our lives. Our insecurity shouts that everyone must follow the same spiritual pathway as we do. Our fears compel us to strive and go on striving.

All our self-effort will never produce spiritual victory. The Holy Spirit alone can achieve that—what is more, he is alive and at work within us. If we will abdicate the throne of our own lives, then he can reign, rule and win in us. What is more, the evidence of that victory will grow daily—as it has, and I praise God, Harry, for all that he has done for you.

There is just one thing left to say—you've seen God begin to work out his purposes in your life. Don't ever stop, keep going, and recognize that in our nation God is raising up an army of ordinary people who will love and serve the living God—whatever the cost.

Postlude

Finally, be strong in the Lord and in his mighty power. Put on the full armour of God so that you can take your stand against the devil's schemes. For our struggle is not against flesh and blood, but against the rulers, against the authorities, against the powers of this dark world and against the spiritual forces of evil in the heavenly realms. Therefore put on the full armour of God, so that when the day of evil comes, you may be able to stand your ground, and after you have done everything, to stand. Stand firm then, with the belt of truth buckled round your waist, with the breastplate of righteousness in place, and with your feet fitted with the readiness that comes from the gospel of peace. In addition to all this, take up the shield of faith, with which you can extinguish all the flaming arrows of the evil one. Take the helmet of salvation and the sword of the Spirit, which is the word of God. And pray in the Spirit on all occasions with all kinds of prayers and requests. With this in mind, be alert and always keep on praying for all the saints.

Ephesians 6:10–18

Ears to Hear

Listening to God and others

by Derek Copley and Mary Austin

Most of us are very good at talking—we've had a lifetime's experience. Day after day we expect others to listen to what we have to say.

But how good are we at *listening?*

This book was born out of the conviction that if we learn how to listen for God's voice, and obey it when we hear it, then we will find a new effectiveness in listening to others. As we learn to show real love and acceptance to others so we will become more like the greatest listener of all, Jesus Christ.

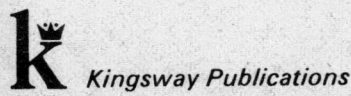

Kingsway Publications

Taking a lead

by Derek Copley

What does it take to be a leader in God's church? Are there principles that apply equally to famous national figures and unknown home group leaders?

> I regard this as essential reading for everyone involved in the care of Christians—no matter at what level. How I wish someone had given me such valuable instruction when I first stepped into the ministry.
>
> —SELWYN HUGHES
> *Director, Crusade for World Revival*

> Derek Copley writes with sensitivity and humility. There is a stubborn honesty about his book... and a constant awareness that leadership is not an end in itself but a means towards the end that the will of God be done.
>
> —JIM GRAHAM
> *Senior Pastor, Goldhill Baptist Church*

> Derek Copley is ideally placed for opening a window onto Christian leadership. As a college principal he works with leaders in the making—and he works from an applied biblical perspective.
>
> —RICHARD BEWES
> *Vicar, All Souls Church, Langham Place*

> Derek Copley sensitively yet challengingly takes up the issues and gives many new and stimulating insights to enable us further in the gift of leading God's people.
>
> —ROGER FORSTER
> *Leader, Ichthus Christian Fellowship*

Derek Copley is Principal of Moorlands Bible College and an elder in his local church.

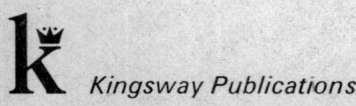

Kingsway Publications

Living God's Way
A Course for Discipling New Christians

by Arthur Wallis

We live in a day of exciting growth, when churches are experiencing a new outpouring of the Holy Spirit and new believers are being gathered in.

The challenge is clear. Christians need to be firmly grounded in the truths of Scripture, so that they are equipped to give teaching and pastoral help to new believers.

This course has been specially designed for use in the local church setting, and is ideal for one-to-one discipling. With a clear and straightforward approach it covers the Bible's basic teaching so that the new Christian can gain a thorough understanding of Christian commitment and how it affects every area of life.

Also in Kingsway paperback by Arthur Wallis:
INTO BATTLE
THE RADICAL CHRISTIAN
PRAY IN THE SPIRIT
GOD'S CHOSEN FAST

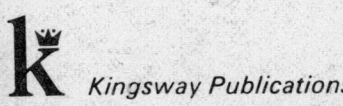

Kingsway Publications

How to Live the Christian Life

by Selwyn Hughes
author of *Every Day with Jesus*

Do you
> *wish the day was over before it has hardly begun?*
> *get irritated by even the smallest problems?*
> *find reading the Bible every day difficult and tiresome?*
> *have trouble mastering temptation?*
> *try to copy others instead of developing your own gifts?*

We can cram our heads with doctrine, but that in itself will not keep us from the problems that rob our lives of the peace, joy and effectiveness that Jesus promised. This book points the way through such problems, helping us to become the kind of people God intended. It is a positive affirmation that we *can* get the best out of the Christian life.

Kingsway Publications

The Father Heart of God

by Floyd McClung

What is God like?

Has he got time for twentieth-century men and women?

Does he really care?

In his work with *Youth with a Mission,* Floyd McClung has met many who suffer from deep emotional hurts and fears.

Time and again it has been the discovery of God as Father—perfect and reliable, unlike any human parent—that has brought healing and liberty.

This book is for you...

...if you find it hard to accept God as a loving father, or
...if you know God's love but would like to share his blessing with others more effectively.

k
Kingsway Publications

Into Battle
A manual of the Christian life

by Arthur Wallis

Every person is involved in a spiritual war. Becoming a Christian is to join forces with God against the powers of darkness.

This book is a battle manual of the Christian life. It shows step by step how to enlist and prepare for action, starting with repentance from sin, faith in the saving power of God and then baptism in water and in the Holy Spirit.

But it does not stop there. The book goes on to show how victory over the enemy can become an increasing reality in every part of our lives.

Other Kingsway paperbacks by Arthur Wallis:

> *The Radical Christian*
> *Pray in the Spirit*
> *God's chosen Fast*

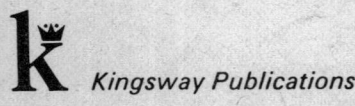

Kingsway Publications